Reading Castaneda
a Prologue to the Social Sciences

David Silverman
Department of Sociology
Goldsmiths' College
University of London

Routledge & Kegan Paul
LONDON AND HENLEY

First published in 1975
by Routledge & Kegan Paul Ltd
39, Store Street
London WC1E 7DD and
Broadway House, Newtown Road
Henley-on-Thames, Oxon RG9 1EN
Set in Monotype Imprint
and printed in Great Britain by
Unwin Brothers Limited
The Gresham Press, Old Woking, Surrey
A member of the Staples Printing Group
© David Silverman 1975

ISBN 0 7100 8145 6 (c)
ISBN 0 7100 8146 4 (p)

Reading Castaneda
a Prologue to the Social Sciences

For Danielle and Andrew,
my daughter and son

Contents

Preface

Sociology rests on a happy irony. It seeks to study socially organized practices. Equally, it itself is inevitably a socially organized practice. Sociological descriptions, methods and claims to truth are brought off and recognized (like lay descriptions, methods and claims to truth) by and for members of a certain community. Their intelligibility resides in the games that each community plays and in the mode of existence which is expressed in playing these games. Necessarily, then, sociological accounts *exemplify* the very practices that they would *describe*. Near at hand, by every such account, stalks the demon of the infinite regress, threatening to push it (and the accounter) down a slope of unending accounts of accounts.

Yet a *happy* irony because a perceived need to counter this threat has produced some of the most significant work in the sociological tradition. To the European sociologists of the early twentieth century, the sociological enterprise could only be justified by establishing a site of difference for the sociologist as compared to the layman. For Durkheim and Weber, the sociologist's claim to difference (deference?) arose in his attempt to seek causally adequate generalizations, putting on one side his societal commitments in favour of the white coat of scientific objectivity. To some modern sociologists, on the other hand, the only possible basis for knowledge of social processes resided in the sociologist's membership of society. Rather than overcome that membership, he must seek to explicate it; for instance by examining how, despite the threat of an infinite regress, intelligible accounts are produced for the practical purposes at hand.

Unfortunately, one does not always study one's own society: sometimes the games that other communities play are unintelligible, and reference to what is taken for granted in your own society seems to be no use. In coming to grips with the socially organized practices of other societies, the sociologist or anthropologist displays most clearly the nature of his method. By continuously settling the issue of what is to count as an adequate description or explanation of social processes – what the native informant tells you, what you understand as a member of another society, what is to be established by social science concepts or quantitative measures – the researcher reveals his version of analysis.

One merit of Carlos Castaneda's accounts of his meetings with the Yaqui Indian magician don Juan is that the reader is continually brought face-to-face with the socially organized practices that constitute not only don Juan's world but also his own. Partly, this reflects Castaneda's honesty in expressing his own doubts and uncertainties rather than offering a polished but empty scientific paper. Partly, it is a feature of don Juan's often exasperating opaqueness, expressed in an apparent failure to clarify even what seems to be the most simple issue. Together with Castaneda, then, we learn that making sense together is not an easy affair and that whatever sense we do make involves a commitment to play a particular game. Because such problems seem to thrust themselves at us here, unlike the more familiar products of the social science community, Castaneda's accounts provide a fitting occasion to re-view the basis of the sociological enterprise.

There is no requirement, however, to read Castaneda's trilogy of books (*The Teachings of Don Juan, A Separate Reality, Journey to Ixtlan*) in order to follow my argument. For the sake of simplicity, all the passages I have quoted are taken from the first book, while, in each chapter, Castaneda's text is used only as an initial springboard to more general issues. Suffice it to say that the books tell of the conversations and experiences of a California anthropology student during ten years of meetings with the circle of an old

Mexican Indian, and of the former's attempts to understand the latter's way of knowledge.

Two final points of clarification: (1) This does not seek to be an addition to the 'drug literature', assuming that such a corpus of texts exists. While Castaneda is introduced to a variety of hallucinogenic materials during the period of his 'apprenticeship' to don Juan, this book does not enter into the debate about the 'effects' of such drug use. Put crudely, I believe that more important issues are at stake here (and this seems to be recognized by both major protagonists). (2) It does not matter to me in the least whether any or all of the 'events' reported by Castaneda ever 'took place'. I have seen some contradictory 'factual' evidence and there is also the issue of the apparent and curious similarity between don Juan's utterances and those of one or two contemporary philosophers. Yet what text is not a construction? To take Castaneda's text seriously seems to require us to bracket the question of its correspondence to any particular set of 'events'.

A version of this book was offered in a series of lectures given in the Department of Sociology, University of California, Los Angeles, in 1973 and I should like to express my thanks to the students present whose questions contributed in no small measure to this work. Alan Dawe, Barry Sandywell and Brian Torode read portions of an earlier draft, and I am most grateful for their comments. I would like to thank the University of California Press for permission to quote extracts from *The Teachings of Don Juan* (University of California Press, 1968). For convenience, the page references in my text refer to the Penguin edition of Castaneda's book.

D. S.

1
Reading Castaneda

For the sake of the argument that I want to advance, let us say that there are two kinds of introduction to a subject. The first emphasizes substance; it provides a kind of package tour of the major concepts and theories. The beginning student, it is hoped, will gain an overview of the subject as a whole, an overview that will allow him to understand more advanced courses, if he should choose, or will 'fill him in' sufficiently for him to relate the subject area to a more major interest.

The second emphasizes what it is to reason in the manner of the discipline and aims at the joint participation of writer and reader in negotiating the character of that reasoning.

As you may have gathered from the way in which I have worded these alternatives, I prefer the latter. Learning substance, as an end in itself, allocates an essentially passive role to the reader. It makes him the mere recipient of a cluster of facts, a kind of empty box into which information has to be pumped. Put bluntly (and unfairly to the rejected alternative), what matters in a first exposure to a subject is the encounter between reader and text – not learning exactly what X said and how it relates to Y's opinions. What matters, fundamentally, is *thinking together* (where that 'together' need not relate to the physical presence of others but to the others that are always present with us in our language, in our history).

So *The Teachings of Don Juan*, as well as any self-proclaimed sociological material that you may come across, is, for our present purposes, less significant for its substance (as if words on a page could have substance!), than for what *you* make of it. By this I mean that you should not be afraid to take seriously your reaction to a book, a lecture or a film. It is *your* reaction and even should it elicit comments about being ill-informed, naïve, or whatever, this cannot make it any less your own. However, as I will be arguing, our reactions (and the selves which they express) are never entirely personal. Our identities are expressions of our common humanity as that humanity is re-membered in particular communities at particular historical epochs. Indeed, the very language of our reactions cannot be private for it makes sense to others even though they have no way of reading our mind. So even as we voice a deeply personal opinion, we are giving expression to our membership within language, within community. Through and through, our selves are public.

To take a trivial example. When I come out of a cinema, I usually hear talk all around me which seems to relate to people's reactions to the movie. Even though I don't know the speakers or will ever meet them, I can immediately assign such a sense to comments like: 'I didn't like it because . . .' or, 'Well it didn't get very good reviews but it was really funny (sad) (true to life) . . .'. Now, of course, context is always crucial for making sense of any activity. Imagine the comments I have given above being given in apparent reply to a question such as: 'How are you feeling today?' or, 'How do you get on with Professor X?'; or someone emerging from a cinema and being overheard to say: 'Very tasty – I must eat there again'!

Of course, if pushed, we could all make some sense out of these kinds of remarks in the course of a conversation. In making that sense, we would be imagining the kind of context in which such a remark would be sensible. Further, in hearing it as a remark rather than, say, an insult or a greeting, we would be exemplifying our ability to recognize an instance as simply an instance. To recognize that 'something is happening' rather than 'nothing is happening', is already to find ourselves deeply within language, within community. And this holds equally for our own speech and other activities as well as for our ability to make sense of the activities of others. So in locating contexts, understanding instances of particular kinds and in recognizing that 'something is happening', we display our membership of society, our public competences. Which is not to say we cannot think our own thoughts, think differently, but rather that own-ness, difference, is only possible within community.

When I ask you to take your reaction 'seriously', then, I do not simply mean that you should maintain it against all-comers. For this is simply stubbornness. To take one's speech seriously can also mean to consider how its private character is available to you as a member of a public community. For instance, how your reaction to a movie could still be recognized by me as a possible intelligible reaction. As a reaction with which I might disagree but which, none the less, I might (but perhaps did not) have myself. As an utterance which allows me to formulate some sense of your intentions, your meaning, without my possessing any other way to get inside your head.

As I read Castaneda's account of his initial conversations with don Juan, I sensed his incomprehension, even anger, at don Juan's replies to his questions. Given the apparently opaque character of don Juan's answers, it is an incomprehension with which any person reared on the Western way of knowledge can fully sympathize. But we need not just see the good sense of Castaneda's reactions, nor, in the patronizing manner which it expresses, need we say of don Juan's knowledge 'how interesting', 'how quaint', and then pass on. For this would be to fit a profoundly challenging way of knowledge into what we already take for granted; to render the unknown known, the incomprehensible comprehensible. Instead, we might consider the character of Castaneda's incomprehension. We might use the 'difficulty' of don Juan's answers as an occasion to interrogate our own system of rationality. An occasion to probe what we routinely take to be comprehensible, to be familiar.

For familiarity is usually only recognized by its absence. The experience of unfamiliar settings can make us recollect the taken form of granted familiarity of everyday situations, which, by comparison with what we now experience, seem on reflection, to be amazingly obvious and non-problematic. Now of course, the 'unfamiliar' is relative to persons' recognition of situations. Engage in an activity repeatedly and its features become routine. Then you will hardly recognize that what is happening around you (and with your participation) is *an* activity and is *that* activity. The situation is, as it were, seen but unnoticed. Think, for instance, about your first day at school or at work and how quickly its unfamiliarity was lost from your attention. So, if one is concerned with what counts as knowledge within our community, we must seek for occasions which make unfamiliar that which we already know and hence have taken for granted. That is why don Juan's way of knowledge, if addressed seriously, provides an occasion to interrogate our way of knowledge.

Castaneda's confusion

Two-thirds of the way through the book, Castaneda reports a conversation with don Juan. He has just smoked a mixture of ingredients (don Juan's ally – the 'little smoke') and, as usual, begins to describe his impressions:

> 'I really felt I had lost my body, don Juan.'
> 'You did.'
> 'You mean, I really didn't have a body?'
> 'What do *you* think yourself?'
> 'Well, I don't know. All I can tell you is what I felt.'
> 'That's all there is in reality – what you felt.'
> 'But how did you see me, don Juan? How did I appear to you?'
> 'How I saw you does not matter . . .'
> . . . 'But I had my body, didn't I, although I couldn't feel it?'
> 'No! Goddammit! You did not have a body like the body you have today!'
> 'What happened to my body then?'
> 'I thought you understood. The little smoke took your body.'
> 'But where did it go?'
> 'How in hell do you expect me to know that?'
> It was useless to persist in trying to get a 'rational' explanation. I told him I did not want to argue or to ask stupid questions, but if I accepted the idea that it was possible to lose my body I would lose all my rationality. (pp. 138-9)

How are we to understand Castaneda's confusion? (1) Castaneda seems confused by the absence of any apparent way of establishing 'what really happened' when he smoked the 'little smoke'. Notice how he uses the term 'really' in the first question of this exchange ('You mean, I *really* didn't have a body?'). He wants don Juan to tell him what really happened. Yet don Juan seems evasive and there seems to be no line of questioning which will elicit for Castaneda the 'facts of the case'. (2) Don Juan keeps on insisting that Castaneda's own experience is central ('That's all there is in reality – what you felt') and that a second party's observations are irrelevant – or, rather, that they make their *own* sense but cannot replace Castaneda's experiences themselves. Yet in our everyday life we rely on others giving us their opinions when we think we might be mistaken. To be told 'How I saw you does not matter' seems to indicate that the speaker is being deliberately difficult. (3) Don Juan fails to concede to Castaneda that, in the midst of even considerable uncertainty, some things can always be relied upon. The world may seem strange sometimes but if you cannot count on remaining in your body, then strangeness becomes utter confusion ('. . . if I accepted the idea that it was possible to lose my body I would lose all my rationality'). (4) One of the things upon which we count, even in strange situations, is that, perhaps only at some time in the future, we could locate an identifiable cause for a recognizable effect. Such causes will be acceptable if they seem to fit the 'facts of the case' and to be in accord with what everyone knows about time and place. Yet don Juan will not help Castaneda in defining the facts of the case, neither will he provide an acceptable cause for Castaneda's peculiar experience. What can it mean to say 'The little smoke took your body', in terms of how either a scientist or the man-in-the-street takes account of the laws of nature? Utterly confused, Castaneda can only break off the conversation ('It was useless to persist in trying to get a "rational" explanation'). Instead of aid, he has received only further troubles; instead of enlightenment, only deeper confusion.

Castaneda's problem

Castaneda's problems with understanding don Juan's teachings relate to the kind of concerns that he brought with him. On the one hand, he wanted to write an acceptable anthropological study. On the other hand, he faced increasingly the practical problem

B

of understanding and getting by that anyone experiences when
encountering a new order of knowledge (the teachings of a *brujo*
(or magician), sociology, baby-care). Perhaps the two concerns,
academic and practical, ultimately merge for him as he tries to
assent that he can make a sense out of don Juan's teachings. For,
if he cannot, he would class himself not only as a non-anthropologist
but, more seriously, as a non-member, someone without the basic
social competences involved in membership of some society. To
accept this is to go out of one's mind – to 'lose all my rationality'.
Yet, even given all the rewards of 'knowledge' (and the dangers of
ignorance), Castaneda experiences great difficulty in making sense
of don Juan's order of knowledge:

> To discover that order and to understand it proved to be a
> most difficult task for me. My inability to arrive at an under-
> standing seems to have been traceable to the fact that, after
> four years of apprenticeship, I was still a beginner. (p. 19)

Let me formulate Castaneda's problem in terms of a two-fold
question. First, *how* do you find out? What methods work: trial
and error, instruction, or what? Second, *what* do you find out?
How things are related to one another? But what if 'things' are
not as you had understood them and 'relationships' (e.g. between
the little smoke and losing one's body) seem nonsense? Towards
the beginning of his conversations, Castaneda prods don Juan
into revealing some of his teachings. Yet, in the ensuing attempt
to discover his 'spot', Castaneda finds only bewilderment. He is
only told that a spot is a place on the floor where he could sit
without fatigue but he has no idea about how he should proceed
to locate it, nor is he clear about what a 'spot' looks like. He learns
further that a 'spot' is a place where a man feels naturally happy
and strong and that don Juan is sitting on his own spot; but his
attempts to find his 'spot' are greeted by protests from don Juan
and, eventually, annoyance and accusations that he had not listened,
perhaps because he did not really want to learn. When told that
he has found his 'spot', Castaneda is no clearer about what he
has really found, nor about how he found 'it':

> It was not clear to me whether or not I had solved the problem,
> and, in fact I was not even convinced that there had been a

problem; I could not avoid feeling that the whole experience
was forced and arbitrary. (p. 36)

So Castaneda's problem is more than just 'how to do it' – a
problem with which we are routinely faced in everyday life and
which we routinely resolve by learning and applying *techniques*.
His problem, as he states it, is that it is by no means certain that
he has a problem; yet another person insists that he has. Since
he wants to learn that man's knowledge, he must guess how to do
'it', without even knowing what 'it' is.

Now to be troubled but not to be sure what is troubling you
and to suspect that it might be nothing at all, is not how we
routinely experience the everyday world. To take his troubles
seriously, as seems necessary to understand don Juan's teachings,
Castaneda must let go the certainties of his mundane existence.
Yet, in doing so, he risks losing what he conceives to be 'all his
rationality'. He continually finds himself in situations where his
only certainty is that somewhere there are unknown means to
achieve undisclosed ends. For instance, some time after the 'spot'
incident, Castaneda is using *datura* paste:

> I rubbed my temples eleven times, without noticing any effect.
> I tried very carefully to take account of any change in per-
> ception or mood, for I did not even know what to anticipate.
> As a matter of fact, I could not conceive the nature of the
> experience, and kept on searching for clues. (p. 114)

Once again, he finds himself playing the self-evidently crazy
game of searching for 'clues' when he has no idea of what he is
looking for ('. . . I did not even know what to anticipate . . . I
could not conceive the nature of the experience'). To make
matters worse, when Castaneda feels he is making some progress
(to who knows where), he is frequently scolded by don Juan for
not listening or seeing properly. For instance, after he has per-
formed some operations with lizards who, don Juan assures him,
will tell him anything that he could not find out for himself, he
is reprimanded:

> 'Next time you must listen carefully. I am sure the lizards told
> you many, many things but you were not listening.' (p. 117)

It is perhaps instructive to compare Castaneda's problem to the problems we encounter in trying to interpret the more opaque features of certain events. When we view what we take to be a 'difficult' film or play, we may come out asking: 'What really happened?' And we have a real problem – *how* to find out? But our problem is by no means as deep as Castaneda's. For at least we know *what* we want to find out – the story, the fashionable opinion, the director's intentions, etc. Our membership of society already makes available to us such areas of knowledge as reasonable ends of enquiry. By already knowing the character of reasonable enquiry for our society, we can safely pose questions and find answers that make sense. By gathering information, we use and sustain our way of knowledge. But what if the way to knowledge is itself the concern of our questions? If we seek, not fresh information, secure in the mode of understanding that allows us to generate and recognize it, but a fresh way of seeing?

Perhaps then we feel trapped in a vicious circle. For our understandings of another way of knowledge can only be from within our own way of knowledge. Our interrogation of the other way is already located within our way. To enter fully into that other way is not simply to learn new techniques or to gather more information. It is rather to adopt the model of reasonable enquiry which the way of knowledge provides. In seeking to understand how to do 'it', Castaneda must ask the kinds of questions which Yaqui knowledge allows to be asked of itself. In finding out what 'it' is, he must recognize that 'it' only arises through the adoption of what counts as a method of reasonable enquiry – which, in characterizing the world, constitutes the world (for the purposes of its investigation).

Now of course Castaneda could have offered an account of don Juan's teachings which would have seemed satisfying to many readers (both lay and professional) precisely because it did not raise such issues. He could have 'described' the 'strange' character of Yaqui knowledge in such a way as to make it seem entirely manageable within our routine categories for ordering such things (norm, value, culture) and, thereby, entirely unchallenging to our mode of reasonable enquiry. Yet he does not – at least in my reading of his book. In refusing the easy option of a glossary of don Juan's teachings, which would present the impression of a

writer who had everything under his control, Castaneda elects to
speak seriously. For if gossiping or chatting characterizes the
unthinking adoption of a tradition of enquiry, speaking seriously
points towards an enterprise which elects to use each and every
topic as an occasion to address the character of enquiry, most specifically its own enquiry. In this way, an analysis of Castaneda's
concrete problems (how to do 'it', what 'it' is) can help us come
to grips with the recurrent issues that face us each time we want
to speak seriously, to Say rather than to chatter.

I have chosen to discuss Castaneda's book, then, because his
problems of incomprehension disturbed him sufficiently for him
to want to address the tradition of enquiry which had constituted
the character of the world for him. This was not an easy path
for him, and on many occasions he became angry and wanted to
give up. In this respect, we might listen to the words of the contemporary German philosopher, Martin Heidegger:

> To the common comprehension, the incomprehensible is never
> an occasion to stop and look at its own powers of comprehension,
> still less to notice their limitations. To the common comprehen-
> sion, what is incomprehensible remains merely *offensive* – proof
> enough to such comprehension which is convinced it was born
> comprehending everything, that it is now being imposed upon
> with a sham. The one thing of which sound common sense is
> least capable is acknowledgment and respect. (1968, pp. 76-7)

Respecting the incomprehensible

If we are not convinced that we were born knowing everything
and do not, therefore, find the incomprehensible offensive, what
might there be about the incomprehensible which would merit
acknowledgment and respect? What issues might confront us if,
like Castaneda, the incomprehensible should give us an occasion
to speak seriously? The topics that arise for me I will index by
the words 'description', 'method', 'truth' and 'reading'. Each of
these topics will be considered sequentially in the chapters that
follow. Yet this choice of topics is not arbitrary. In speaking to
them, I define what 'baggage' of ideas I carry around with me.
So the organization of this book (like that of any book) is its
author's confession. It confesses his claim to speak seriously; it

confesses himself. So, whether discussing 'description', say, or 'method', my text itself exemplifies what it is to describe and to be methodical.

I want to introduce these issues now but will do so largely by mentioning some of the questions that each raised for me as I read *The Teachings of Don Juan*.

1. *Description*   What is it to offer a description of something? How do descriptions relate to the 'things' which they describe? What work do descriptions do? Are they verbal photographs: what does it mean to say that descriptions represent the world? What is the relation between the dictionary definition of a word and its use? For Castaneda this is the problem of what a 'spot' or any other object of don Juan's world *is*. Castaneda just wants don Juan to describe these objects so that he can learn more rapidly. This don Juan always seems to avoid doing. How can an understanding of 'description' help us in understanding what seems to be don Juan's stubbornness or evasiveness?

2. *Method/Rule*   What do methods do for us? Are they rules for instructing us what to do in order to achieve a desired end? What does it look like to follow a rule? How do we know when to apply the rule? Can there be rules for the application of rules? What is it like to learn a method? For Castaneda, this is the problem of *how* you find out. He seems to want recipes for success from don Juan, yet surprisingly few are forthcoming. Why?

3. *Truth*   What makes an assertion true? Do true assertions 'copy' reality? Are true ideas those we cannot refute? How does truth relate to perception? What is the relation between language and truth? Is truth simply what people happen to take to be true? For Castaneda, this is the problem of finding out what was 'really' happening to him. Did he really fly, really become a crow? Why does don Juan tell him to trust his own experience? What is 'the reality of special consensus' and how does it relate to the truth of assertions for don Juan and for us?

4. *Reading*   What is it to 'understand' a statement? Is it to grasp the author's intentions? And where do these intentions reside – in

what he says in a preface or when talking about his work else-
where or only in the text alone? What is the status of the reader's
understandings versus the author's intentions? Can (should) the
author define how his book should be read? Is the audience a
passive receptacle for the words of the author? Is it a judge?
Does criticism imply disagreement or difference? For Castaneda,
this is the problem of reporting don Juan's teachings for us.
What happens when he seeks to grasp Yaqui knowledge? Does his
book (and his 'structural analysis') 'describe' the teachings? What
does my account 'describe'?

What is the relation between the words of a speaker and himself
or a person who is a member (of society)? What does it look like
to claim a separation between fact and value, between objectivity
and subjectivity? What allows us to see 'bias' as a problem which
gets in the way of proper description, prevents truth and is
improperly methodical? For Castaneda, this is the problem of
explaining Yaqui knowledge as a member of a different community to that community. For don Juan, the issue of responsible
reading is understood differently. The aim is to find a path 'with
heart'. Finding it and understanding it is your task, yet you
cannot find it without already being a competent member. So to
'find out' re-members membership. There is no neutral path to
knowledge. Even to find out 'about' membership is itself insepar-
able from membership.

These and other issues I will address in the pages that follow.
At this stage I only want to make two further points. The first
relates to sociology, the second to expertise.

So far what I have written may read to some audiences as more
like philosophy than sociology. There is no way of knowing. Take
it as you like. All I want to do here is to assert the social and
public character of the issues to which I have referred *and* of
my writing and your reading 'about them'. Rather than being
individual and private matters, 'description', 'method', 'truth',
and 'reading' are always through and through, inescapably,
socially organized practices. By 'socially organized practice'
I refer to each and every occasion where communal rules are
invoked for recognizing and sanctioning a course of action. Such
invocation is entirely a social matter. It occurs because membership is expressed in the competences required to invoke a rule.

In its occurrence, it guarantees the orderly character of the world as members understand it. If, then, sociology takes as its topic the socially organized practices that produce the orderly character of the world (social order), you could well be reading sociology. I say 'could well' because I am already deep in the territory of reading and this is a topic that will be left until later.

About expertise. In referring to the quote from Heidegger and his mention of 'the common comprehension', it might have seemed that I was both trying to put you down and claiming a special competence (expertise) for myself. The expert is a person who claims (and is granted) special mastery over the language of technique and (sometimes) over the technique of language (rhetoric). Yet this book provides no techniques, nor is it written to convince you – in the sense that your entry into the book does not have to be through the claims which I make about it, e.g. as sociology or philosophy. As I began by saying, your reaction is necessarily your own. But this means that you are responsible for it, for the tradition which your reading exemplifies, for the community you collect yourself into through its expression.

Neither of us, however, is on his own. Both writer and reader are engaged in a co-operative enterprise. In writing, I forget what makes writing possible – as Castaneda, in questioning, forgets what makes his questions possible. I need you, as Castaneda needs a reader, to formulate the way of knowledge that makes my writing intelligible. And that formulation will itself be an act of production – a reading that is also always a writing. But I reach ahead of myself.

2
Description

Describe – To represent by words, give an account of ...
(*Webster's Collegiate Dictionary*, fifth edition)

It is almost embarrassing to refer to a dictionary for a definition of 'describe'. After all, 'describe' is a word we use all the time. Not to know how to use it is to suggest a kind of unfamiliarity with everyday life that we would attribute to foreigners or madmen. Further, and more relevant for our purposes, in turning to a dictionary, we presuppose a competence in understanding descriptions. After all, what does a dictionary do, if not to provide 'descriptions' of everyday usage? So to understand any dictionary definition (including that of 'describe'), it is always necessary to know already what it is to describe. What kind of activity is an enquiry which presupposes that we know already?

To pose such a question, for me, goes to the heart of Castaneda's 'troubles'. For, as we make enquiries of whatever kind, we trade off some model of reasonable enquiry which grounds the 'good sense' of both our questions and answers. The difficulty and danger of Castaneda's path, the risk of losing 'all his rationality', arises, in my reading, as he is tormented by this understanding. There is *no* kind of enquiry which does not presuppose that we know already.

Yet all Castaneda's 'rationality' turns him away from such an understanding. In his dialogues with don Juan, he continually

seeks to learn *more* about his experiences, as if his very consciousness of experience did not guarantee his commitment to a model
of reasonable enquiry which, in my terms, he knew already.
Notice, in the following passage, his search for *further* 'information' despite his suspicion that he was not going to get it:

> There was a question I wanted to ask him. I knew he was
> going to evade it, so I waited for him to mention the subject;
> I waited all day. Finally, before I left that evening, I had to
> ask him, 'Did I really fly, don Juan?' (p. 128)

Castaneda senses that don Juan is going to 'evade' his question.
As becomes clear shortly, his prediction seems to be correct, for
he is baffled and confused by don Juan's responses. However,
there remains the issue of why Castaneda's question ('Did I
really fly, don Juan?') should make sense to us and, consequently,
why don Juan's replies should seem like 'evasions'. To address
this issue, I shall return to the dictionary definition already cited.

If to 'describe' is 'to represent by words', then it would seem
that words represent 'things'. A sense of this is to be found in
what we understand as 'representational art' – a convention in
terms of which a painting, say, seeks (or is taken) to represent
'reality'. If this kind of art seems to represent (to picture, to
mirror) reality, then, if we follow the dictionary, a verbal description refers to a set of words which picture or mirror reality.

Now this notion of description provides us with a way of
retrieving the good sense of the question: 'Did I really fly?'
Castaneda has taken what don Juan calls 'the devil's weed' and,
seemingly under its 'influence', has had an experience of flying,
which, in terms of everyday understandings, seems strange and/or
unreal. Consequently, he wonders whether he was deluded. If
we now call what 'actually' happened to Castaneda 'reality', then
we can see that his problem is whether his account *accurately*
pictures or mirrors reality. In short, is it a 'good' or a 'bad'
description of the 'things' that 'really' happened to him?

One way of settling whether a description is good or bad,
unbiased or biased, is to ask a second party. This person should
preferably have witnessed the 'thing' that happened (especially in
a situation where, unlike us, he was not at the time under the
influence of a hallucinogenic drug) so that his account will provide

a crucial test of the accuracy of ours. Hence: 'Did I really fly, don Juan?'

An additional basis for intelligibly asking such a question is that, not only did don Juan witness 'what happened', but that, as a *brujo*, don Juan seems like just the man to ask. It is as if we were to ask a question of a surgeon who had been present at our operation or a bridge master who had watched us play out a hand. In all these cases, our confidence in the information that we expect to be given is rooted securely in our knowledge that our informant both witnessed the event and, anyway, is to be regarded as an *expert* in events-of-this-nature. Yet, as Castaneda says he knew before he asked the question, don Juan will not proffer the appropriate information:

'Did I really fly, don Juan?'
'That is what you told me. Didn't you?' (*ibid.*)

What kind of answer can this be? Castaneda, after all, only wants to know whether his account accurately described what happened. As an expert, it should be don Juan's role to 'correct' Castaneda's impressions and to describe the 'facts of the case'. Yet he just points out to Castaneda that: 'That is what you told me. Didn't you?' No check, no test, no alternative account.

I suppose one way of reading don Juan's response is in terms of non-directional therapy as used in psycho-analysis. Here the analyst will never be drawn to offer his own comments and always throws any question back to his patient. Alternatively, we could read his remark as an indication of obstinacy or of deliberate concealment – perhaps, we might surmise, don Juan is intentionally trying to make things difficult for his apprentice. But what if we locate the 'difficulty' within our (Castaneda's) way of knowledge? If we respect the 'incomprehensible' and use it as an occasion to interrogate our own way of knowledge?

Clearly, as we understand it, second parties, whether witnesses or experts, help us in testing the accuracy of our impressions. Let us call this the Second Party Assumption. So don Juan's insistence on the integrity and self-sufficiency of Castaneda's impressions strikes us as obstinate because, unlike us, as he understands it, witnesses or experts have no relevance for personal experience. For him, it would seem, it is personal experience which counts and which, whatever others may tell us, must be preserved, although, as I shall argue shortly, experience is never uniquely your own, never private.

Of course, this is not at all the way in which Castaneda seems to read don Juan's reply. For he poses the further question:

'I know, don Juan, I mean, did my body fly? Did I take off like a bird?' (*ibid.*)

I take the force of Castaneda's comment 'I know' to reside in an assumption that don Juan has *misunderstood* the purpose of the question. Of course, Castaneda knows that he had the 'experience' of flying. But his question did not refer to that experience but to what 'really' happened – 'I mean, did my body fly? Did I take off like a bird?' What 'really' happened, as opposed to personal 'experience', Castaneda assumes, is available to any competent witness.

We can see now that the Second Party Assumption rests upon an important distinction between 'experience' and what 'really' happens. To take it seriously, we must assume that, while people can have different experiences, there is at all times a separate body of facts ('what really happened') which exist quite apart from any one person's impressions and, indeed, can be used to check the accuracy of experience. This is the distinction, long familiar to thought, between subject and object and, as expressed in accounts, between subjectivity and objectivity.

So, according to this reading, don Juan's initial response ('That is what you told me. Didn't you?') is treated by Castaneda as, improperly, referring to the world of experience – the subject world ('I know, don Juan'). Instead, he wants don Juan to pay attention to 'what really happened'. Notice how Castaneda's reply stresses his concern with the object world through its emphasis on physical objects: 'I mean, did my *body* fly? Did I take off like a bird?' [my emphasis]. I will call this assumption of an object world, and the distinction between it and the subject world which the assumption gives rise to, the Object World Assumption.

Of course, once again Castaneda does not get the reply he wants, even after having sought to correct what he takes to be don Juan's misreading of his initial question. After Castaneda's second question, don Juan responds:

'You always ask me questions I cannot answer. You flew.
That is what the second portion of the devil's weed is for.'
(*ibid*.)

He goes on to point out that to 'fly' in this way is not to fly as a
bird but to fly 'as a man who has taken the weed'.

For yet another time, Castaneda is thrown off balance. What
can it possibly mean to fly 'as a man who has taken the weed'?
Since clearly it is not to fly like a bird, perhaps, once again, don
Juan may have misunderstood the purpose of the line of questioning. Perhaps he is simply referring to the world of personal
experience – the subject world. In this way, we can read a sense
of Castaneda's next comment:

'Then I didn't really fly, don Juan. I flew in my imagination,
in my mind alone. Where was my body?' (*ibid*.)

Notice the distinction that we can read into Castaneda's statement between object world ('fly') and subject world ('imagination').
Each is counterposed to the other, as if speech which does not
refer to one must refer to the other. The sentences seem, almost
necessarily, linked: 'Then I didn't really fly, don Juan. [Hence] I
flew in my imagination, in my mind alone.' Yet it is more than a
simple linkage of alternative possibilities. Look at how the adverb
'really' is used when referring to flying but not to 'imagination'
or 'mind'. It is as if experience is not 'really' real for Castaneda.
The object world alone seems to possess for him that quality of
facticity, of being 'really' real. And it is to that object world that
he wishes the conversation to return – 'Where was my body?'
Once again, he tries to clarify his purpose in the face of don
Juan's apparent 'misunderstanding'. Once again, in his terms, he
gets nowhere:

'Where was my body?'
'In the bushes.' (*ibid*.)

Castaneda writes that he found this reply 'cutting', and notes
how don Juan broke into laughter afterwards. But, not to be put
down, the questioner persists. His next tactic is to switch away from
don Juan's observations, by now obviously an unfruitful area,
towards another line of questioning, prefaced by a recognition of
the unfamiliarity of a Yaqui way of knowledge:

'You see, don Juan, you and I are differently oriented. Suppose, for the sake of argument, one of my fellow students had been here with me when I took the devil's weed. Would he have been able to see me flying?' (*ibid.*)

Here, rather than asking don Juan for his view of 'what really happened', Castaneda has invented a hypothetical example. The strength of the example lies in its recognition that, if one is interested in ascertaining 'the facts of the case', a 'neutral' observer (like a fellow-student) will not have the strange 'biases' that seem built into don Juan's perceptions of reality. Further, the example is appealing because what I will call the Hypothetical Example Assumption – whereby one engages in mental experiments as a rule-of-thumb, speedy method of considering hypotheses – is a routine technique through which scientists question the conclusions which common sense seems to suggest. By employing this technique, Castaneda can be viewed as exemplifying the 'critical' spirit of scientific enquiry. If nothing else, at least he seems to be a good scientist.

Don Juan's initial reply suggests yet another failure of comprehension:

'There you go again with your questions about what would happen if . . . . It is useless to talk that way.' (*ibid.*)

In don Juan's way, the Hypothetical Example Assumption makes no sense ('It is useless to talk that way'). Yet the impasse which this implies is, for me, crucially by-passed by an assertion that don Juan makes a little later:

'If your friends knew about men flying with the devil's weed, then they would agree.' (p. 129)

The sense I draw from this is as follows. (1) The Hypothetical Question Assumption posits that a mental experiment and/or a purportedly 'neutral' observer can re-arrange facts in order to test a hypothesis. Yet the re-arrangement of facts is itself a feature of a way of knowledge which provides for the recognition of facts as 'facts'. The 'facts' of the case are not self-constituting, they are not separate from our modes of understanding, but features of it. (2) It follows that what we understand as 'experience' is no more intrinsically 'subjective' than what we recognize as a 'fact' is 'objective'. Both 'experiences' and 'facts' are recognizable and account-able as warranted 'things' of which our language allows us to speak. The 'experience' of flying, equally as well as the 'fact' of flying, is only to be recognized and validated through our language. (3) To speak is to locate oneself within a way of knowledge. To speak is to display one's membership of some society. Hence we are able to recognize experiences, find out facts and check assertions because we know *already*, as members of some language community, what it is (properly) to do all these things. So to see as a Yaqui sees is to see men fly with the devil's weed. And there is no *'neutral'* way of testing this assertion. For not to see men fly with the devil's weed is simply not to see the Yaqui way ('If your friends knew about men flying with the devil's weed, then they would agree').

The conclusion I take from this is that experience is never personal or private. 'Experience', no less than 'facts', is recognized and warranted by the public language of a community. If, then, Castaneda's experiences must be preserved rather than demolished, it is not because they are uniquely his alone. For the validity which they possess for him, they also exhibit for us as common members of his community. That is to say that we can understand Castaneda because we play the same games with language, and our ability to play such games exemplifies our membership of society. To demolish his experiences – to find them naïve, misguided, or whatever – would be to fail to respect the social being that we share with him. To preserve them – to take them seriously – can be to re-member the mode of existence that sustains both our experience and his.

Basic to that experience, and informing both the Second Party and Hypothetical Question assumptions, is what we take to be the intrinsic subjectivity of individual understandings relative to the intrinsic objectivity of the factual world. Graphically, we can depict this hierarchy of knowledge and the distinction upon which it is formed, as in Table 1.

According to Table 1, the Object World – 'the way things are' – is both distinct from our consciousness and provides the basis for testing the validity of what our consciousness tells us. The Subject

World is only 'the way we see things' where those 'things' exist
separately from, and outside, the seeing.

In order to examine the character of this distinction and its
consequences for the nature of 'description', I want to take a
hypothetical example – although, as I have already suggested,
this way of reasoning which I (you?) share with Castaneda, itself
reflects the model of reasonable enquiry which our language
expresses. Let us say that a conviction in a murder trial depends
upon the accuracy of the evidence of one witness. The jury are
torn about whether they should accept his evidence. Then,
suddenly, a new piece of evidence is discovered. Unknown to
anyone, someone was making a home movie at the same time and

TABLE I

Distinction	Subject World	Object World
Where it arises	Rests in our conscious-ness – 'the way we see things'	Solid and factual, apart from our consciousness – 'the way things are'
Its status	Expressed in, and through, our accounts	Constitutes itself – it is the Real Thing
Its validity	Our accounts of the Subject World must be tested against 'the way things are'	Is itself the basis of all tests. Since it is 'the way things are', it cannot be invalid

in the same location as the murder. The film is introduced into
evidence and appears to be of good quality. The jury eagerly
anticipate its viewing – at last, they feel, the matter can be settled
once and for all. The witness's account can be compared to the
film and its validity determined by the extent to which it corresponds with the film.

Now I do not want to suggest any doubt that this indeed will
be the outcome. In such a situation a film would probably settle
the matter. I merely want to consider how this 'settling' gets done.
Let us note to begin, that, for the jurors, the witness's account
stands as a description of 'the ways he saw things'. As such its
validity is always open to doubt – subject to the presumed reliability of the witness, the existence of contrary testimony, cor-
roborating material evidence, etc. Now, however, they will have

the opportunity to test more directly the validity of the witness's account by watching the film. Provided that they are satisfied that the film has not been tampered with and that the camera was properly focused, the jurors will orient themselves towards the film as a record of 'the way things were'.

The issue I now want to raise is, no doubt, entirely familiar to lawyers concerned with such matters. Does the film 'speak' for 'itself'? Don't we have to offer descriptions of what it depicts and aren't these descriptions merely 'the way we see things'? Could it be that 'the way things are' simply is a feature of a consensus that may develop, at a particular time, over a particular issue, as to how, for all practical purposes, 'things' should be 'seen'?

Given that objects are not self-descriptive, we can now recognize the similarities between the jury's understandings (of the film) and the witness's understandings (of what he saw of the 'events'). In both cases, the understanding constitutes the character of what will be presumed to have taken place. For instance, any account, by using terms like 'corpse', 'murderer' or 'weapon', imposes a way of seeing that renders visual impressions as a set of events in a case of this kind (e.g. a murder) that, as common-sense members of society, we are already familiar with. It is not that nothing is happening 'on' the film; rather *that* something is happening is constituted by our reporting practices. In rendering an impression as an observable and reportable event, we provide for the character of the event.

We might also reflect that my use of the context of a trial and a courtroom should not obscure the infinite number of ways in which the film in question might be interpreted. For instance, to see the film as a piece of legal evidence is to elect not to see it as a work of art. And it is, of course, intrinsically neither – no more than it is 'really' a film, rather than a decorative object. Or rather, *it comes to be* really one thing on the occasion that we address it by rendering 'it' as one of the 'its' of which, within our language, we may intelligibly speak.

Consider the ways in which we address a Coca-Cola bottle in ordinary circumstances, or when looking at a Warhol picture. Or take the case of a street map. We might just pick it up and look at it out of 'academic' interest or, perhaps, to familiarize ourselves with a new town. In each case, we look for and 'see' different

c

features. Moreover, neither case resembles the kind of 'seeing' that goes on when we turn to the map having discovered that we are desperately lost. What we look for and 'see' is not the pattern of street directions but simply a way out of our difficulties. So our practical-purpose-at-hand constitutes the character of what we see – the occasion of looking provides what shall be seen (to be). Our accounts are, then, as every lawyer knows, persuasive versions of events which, if taken seriously, assemble those events as events-of-a-particular-kind. The centre of interest as I write, the Watergate tapes, will no more settle the character of what really happened than would the movie in my hypothetical example. Rather, persuasive accounts of what the tapes 'really' signify will battle against each other and, in rendering events intelligible, will produce them as events-of-a-particular-kind.

To return to 'description'. What I have been suggesting here is that by describing events through particular terms and conventions of language, we have already explained the events, i.e. rendered them as an intelligible move in some game (ordering, obeying, murdering) of which our language speaks. So our descriptions constitute events.

Now, if you want to deny this, to say that events might stand outside of our descriptions, you are faced with certain dilemmas. First, the character of the world is not self-defined. Events do not speak for themselves. Second (and this is equally true for my assertion), to characterize the world in a particular way (in your case, as 'outside' descriptions), can itself be viewed as a persuasive account. In either case, the world 'itself' remains to be addressed. Even where we should happen to agree about the 'real' character of the world, that very agreement can be viewed as an outcome of the practices through which we come to generate and recognize 'agreement'; and, yet again, we would have said nothing about the world. Or perhaps we would. Perhaps the mistake is to differentiate our accounts from the world. Perhaps our accounts are our world (for us). So, in recognizing 'agreement', in offering 'hypothetical' questions or in asking for the opinion of a second party, we display commitment to, and membership of, our world, our society, our community. It is not that the world can only be grasped by language – so our accounts can be biased, distorted or mistaken – rather the world is already within our language.

Note that I am *not* asserting that the world is how we choose to see it. All of what I have said is, I believe, consistent with our experience of a 'solid', 'factual' and 'objective' world which both resists our projects and is yet the basic area in which they may be attained. Indeed, the character of that 'factual' world gives the social sciences their initial topic. So economists ask how the commodity market affects the price of food and the balance of payments; psychologists question the relation between isolation and suggestibility to previously opposed views; and sociologists examine the link between relative affluence and changes in the class structure of advanced industrial societies. But, as I have suggested, the character of the factual world, which all these studies consider, provides only an *initial* topic. For, in describing the world, social scientists necessarily constitute its character (for them). In getting themselves 'closer' to 'the way things are', they commit themselves to the ways of speaking that their community makes available to them. Hence their descriptions are intelligible and their explanations testable only *within* the language-game which they (tacitly) propose; only *within* the mode of existence in which we recognize and could want to play such games.

Since all that has just been said must apply equally to any account, the grounds of the distinction between lay and scientific accounts, a distinction dearly beloved by many social scientists, now begins to seem clearer. For at least a century, social scientists have sought to make claims about the greater validity of their accounts relative to everyday understandings. What, for instance, you, in your ignorance, took to be wilful naughtiness by a child, the psychologist might show to be linked to inadequate socialization. Moreover, he could validate his claims through experimental designs which are organized so as to 'control' for the distorting effects of other variables.

However, the explanation of events as, for all social scientific purposes, the outcome of inadequate socialization (or whatever), can itself only be a persuasive version (which produces the character) of those events (as events). It is an account which, in this case, speaks the language of the community of social scientists – a language which constitutes the character of both what they look for and what they find. In 'validating' this (or any) account, they would be doing nothing more than showing their commitments to the communal practices through which they generate and recognize agreement. For instance, like any of us, they would terminate their enquiries when, for all practical purposes, nothing more 'of use' could be said – for the time being. However detailed their enquiries, the world would remain to be described.

To illustrate my contention that descriptions and explanations, whether lay or scientific, provide only persuasive versions of the world, let me take a familiar example. Say we were to be concerned with the character of lectures. More specifically, we might ask: In what lie the lecture-like qualities of an occasion? How does a lecture differ from a seminar, interview or casual conversation?

No doubt anyone who had been present at a lecture could produce a list of some kind which might refer to such features as only one person speaking, while the others present seem not to speak but to write down what he says; or to the failure to begin the talk with any usual greeting sequence. However, if I were to press the producer of the list for more and more detail (In what circumstances may others speak?, Is a cough or a groan, speech?, May not greeting sequences sometimes be used? etc., etc.), it would soon become clear that the list could be endless. So the initial persuasive character of the description would only be persuasive because it was offered to an audience who knew already, in the sense that they were familiar with both the language-games of 'lecturing' and 'description'. Further, the endless elaboration of the list would only eventually seem to be a foolish task because we all know that we don't need lists and exhaustive details in order to recognize lectures and to distinguish them from other occasions. We also know, as competent members of our language-community, *when* it makes sense to formulate the character of an occasion. For instance, we do not routinely expect people to stand up and exclaim, in whatever tones they choose: 'It's a lecture!' (seminar, interview, conversation). At such a time, our words may not be seen to provide a description at all, but rather to offer a joke, a distraction, etc. Conversely, what makes a statement into a recognizable, successful description is not whether it is *intended* to represent or picture the world, but rather the socially recognized occasions at which the statement is read (heard) and the game in which it is located as a move. That is to say, that the 'meaning' of our words is a feature of the manner in which our words are treated, not of our intentions. Words get treated as meaning certain things, in context, because we take them to propose a certain kind of game. So we may intend to describe, but on occasions we may be treated as having offered a joke. That treatment constitutes the character of what our words will have had to have been about, although we may negotiate with a hearer with a view to altering his conception of our words from 'the way things were' to 'the way he saw things'. Yet, in turn, whatever the outcome of that negotiation, what is eventually decided will reflect the practices of negotiation. Rather than finally settling 'the way things were', it will be yet another persuasive version of 'the way things will have had to have been'.

One way of reading the conversations between Castaneda and don Juan is as a negotiation of this way. I shall develop this point when I talk about 'special consensus' in Chapter 4 on 'Truth'. A more mundane example from my experience will also serve as an illustration. An American was talking to me, in what I took to be serious terms, about the Stock Market. As I recall it, after talking in general terms, he seemed to begin a personal anecdote. The subsequent talk went something like this:

HE: 'You know my uncle lost his business in the Wall Street crash.'
I: 'Oh, really?'
HE: 'Yes. You see a banker jumped out of a window and fell on his wheelbarrow.'
I: 'Is that right? How terrible!'
(Silence coupled with a confused and embarrassed expression from him.)

At this point, I realized that my understanding of the character of what the American had been saying must have been 'mistaken'. I 'must have been' thinking about something else and missed out on a switch in his talk from 'describing' to 'joking'. His puzzled expression already had convinced me that I had made a 'mistake' before he had said anything else. We need only note here that the character of any talk or piece of writing is constituted by how its sense is negotiated. Accounts always *come to be seen* as descriptions, jokes, etc.; they always come to be seen as 'the way things are (were)'. So the sense of accounts as descriptions or explanations of 'the way things are' is always located *in the seeing*. A seeing which invariably recognizes the sense of an account through recognizing a context for it. A seeing which is always in and through language which allows us to see (constitute) activities as moves in some understandable game.

Yet both laymen and scientists routinely seek to describe and explain the world as if it were not already there, in their accounts. Hence, if, as suggested earlier, the character of the factual social world gives social scientists their initial topic, the manner in which their scientific accounts, in assembling 'the way things are', constitute a possible society *and* confirm a way of knowledge, must be part of the factual social world which is to be investigated. For, whatever their claims to describe accurately and to explain convincingly, there remains the fundamental character of their writings as accounts, and the manner in which accounts re-call the language of a particular community, in a particular historical epoch.

When Marx characterizes 'capitalist' society, he reminds us that the structures of society, of our modes of existence, are always present in, and through, our activities. In doing their 'science', for instance, the political economists of his day express, for Marx, the character of the community in which and for whom they write:

> It should be noted that it is always empirical businessmen we are talking about when we refer to political economists, their scientific confession and existence. (Marx, 1962 edition, p. 149)

Notice how Marx uses the words 'confession' and 'existence' to refer to their writing. The writing of nineteenth-century political economists is, for him, an inextricable feature of the mode of existence of their authors as representatives, even functionaries, of their societies. Their work 'confesses' their concrete commitments to their society and serves to sustain it. Rather than treat their texts as descriptions of society, Marx would have us consider them as, simultaneously, the foundations and the products of society. For him, their writing forgetfully *does* and *is* society.

Similarly, the distinction between Subject and Object Worlds, outlined in Table 1, is recognized by both contemporary scientists and laymen because it is always already there, within their language, within the way of knowledge of their community. Rather than deny the validity of such a distinction, we must address the manner in which all our speech, lay or scientific, inexorably grounds its sense in, and through, the distinctions provided by the way of knowledge which it exemplifies and sustains. So the question we would want to ask of any account would no longer be: Has the account grasped the world correctly? but rather: What is involved in speaking its language?

Summary

There is no way in which any account, including my own, can avoid relying upon and sustaining a persuasive version of the character of the world. In addressing Castaneda's book in the way I have, I have constituted what, for the purposes of my writing, its character 'will have had to have been'. My account does not 'describe' (represent) the book; it constitutes the book – for my text. So what I write for you cannot possibly be 'about' *his* book; it must, at all times be 'about' *my* book – 'about' my commitments to the language of my text. Let my try and summarize for you the character of the theory which I have offered to you as a persuasive version of the grounds of Castaneda's misunderstandings. For the sake of clarity, I offer you a series of numbered points:

1 Words do not represent things. They are not pictures of things, accurate or otherwise. For instance, to say 'Hello' no more pictures a thing, than Castaneda's 'Then I didn't really fly, don Juan' represents a past set of events.
2 The sense of words is not to be found in our intentions but in how our intentions, in context, are read. 'Motive', for instance, does not describe something in our head but rather a way in which others address what might be in our head. So don Juan is certainly 'evasive' but only in so far as his responses 'look that way' in terms of Western understandings of rational discourse.
3 The way in which words are read depends upon the *game* in which they are located and the *move* in the game which they

seem to constitute. As in sport, different games have different moves which provide for the ways in which activities should be recognized. So, if there are games of football, tennis, etc., there are equally games of describing, commanding, enquiring, etc., with different rules for rendering sense of activities or moves. For instance, Castaneda seems to provide that his questions should be read in terms of the tradition of scientific enquiry with which he is familiar. Yet the paths to knowledge with which don Juan seems to be familiar – and the allies and enemies along them – constitute (what strikes Castaneda as) a difficult and confusing response to 'reasonable' questions.

4   It makes sense to play such games because, in playing them, we recognize our-selves and others. The enactment of the game is the enactment of the social order in which we locate ourselves as competent members. So to understand any list of, say, the characteristics of a lecture, is to find one's identity within the way of knowledge of our society. To understand a definition is to know already (that way of knowledge). Because we are competent members, we can also recognize appropriate contexts for applying that definition, even though some of the features on the list might appear to be missing. Imagine explaining to don Juan that a 'proper' description of a particular gathering was as a 'lecture'. If he were not to understand, we would have to fall back on the assertion that he was not seeing and looking 'properly' – just as he asserts that Castaneda did not 'listen carefully' to the lizards. So 'seeing', 'looking' and 'listening' properly exemplify our membership of some community and the location of all our understandings within its way of knowledge.

Let us consider the following statement which will stand as a summary presentation of the version of description which this chapter has been offering:

In an important sense, in the world there *is* no value and there are no murders, tables, houses. But our language is not about *that* world in which there is no value or no tables... That world, the world of raw data, cannot be described for the sense of that world also lies outside of it and the very description of it, likewise, lies outside it. Thereof one really cannot speak. (Kovesi, quoted by Blum in Douglas, 1971, p. 312.)

When Kovesi begins by denying, 'in an important sense', the existence of these objects, I take him to be referring to the conception of the Object World which I have been considering. This conception assumes the existence of an order of things – 'the way things are' – which exists separately from the seeing. Yet, Kovesi implies, things are neither recognizable nor describable outside language. Without language, then, 'there *is* no value and there are no murders, tables, houses', since names constitute the character of objects for us. Indeed, without language, there is even no 'no' – no 'nothing' – since we constitute absence through the categories of language. However, as Kovesi goes on, 'our language is not about *that* world in which there is no value or no tables'. For our language does indeed provide us with a world of objects, and allows us to talk about 'the way things are' and to distinguish this from 'the way we see things'. It is 'about' that world in which words stand for objects and descriptions 'represent by words'. Outside that language, outside that world, there is no-thing. To describe what Kovesi refers to as 'the world of raw data' is not to represent that world but to constitute it as part of our world – 'the sense of that world lies outside of it and the very description of it, likewise, lies outside it'. So to describe 'the world of raw data', is to describe (represent) our world. For 'raw data' does not speak for itself. As to what it 'really is', 'thereof one really cannot speak'. Or, rather, *in speaking* It (1) (the thing 'itself') eludes us, while It (2) (the-thing-as-we-understand-it) is constituted.

In reminding us that the games of our language are (about) our world, Kovesi's words, like much of this chapter, follow in the tradition of the philosopher, Ludwig Wittgenstein. In his later work, notably *Philosophical Investigations*, Wittgenstein shows how the sense of words is located by the language-game with which, on each occasion, we identify them. Words, then, do not picture or represent objects, they express and are understood by the games with which our community is familiar:

> One thinks that one is tracing the outline of the thing's nature over and over again, and one is merely tracing round the frame through which we look at it.
> A *picture* held us captive. And we could not get outside it, for

it lay in our language and language seemed to repeat it to us inexorably. (1969 edition, p. 48^e)

Even as we feel that we have the objects of our enquiry firmly within our grasp, we are merely reiterating, through our language, our community's version of a persuasive account – 'one is merely tracing round the frame through which we look at it'. Like Kovesi, Wittgenstein reminds us that the pictures that descriptions seem to offer are not pictures of 'raw data' but pictures of the workings of our language.

We seem very distant now from the dictionary definition of 'describe' with which this chapter began. Yet, in a sense, we are much closer to it. For all that has been said indicates that the dictionary has got it right: *in our world*, descriptions do, indeed, 'represent by words, give an account of . . .'. What we have been doing is retrieving the 'good sense' of this persuasive version of description within our world.

Part of that 'good sense' can be suggested if we address playfully the word 'represent'. To hear it as 're-present' suggests another sense with which we are less familiar. For, if descriptions re-present by words, then they no longer serve as mirrors but as vehicles which *present again* before our gaze the world in the manner in which we are used to seeing it. So 'description' no longer seems to reflect a world of objects, but to present again to us that world of objects which is always within our language. To 'hear' description in this way, is to address the deep location of all our enquiries within language. It is to speak in a way which 'listens' to its own language.

The Object World again

I suppose one way of reading all that I have written is as gross subjectivism. Since the distinction between the Object and Subject Worlds is deep within our language, it is tempting to assert that any attempt to consider the human construction of the Object World must necessarily lead to an assumption of the primacy of the Subject World, of 'the way we see things'. Still worse, I might be taken to imply that the world is *entirely* a Subject World and that, therefore, what I don't experience doesn't exist, and that

I can even choose what will be real for me. This is the heresy, long known to philosophy, of solipsism.

As I understand solipsism, it has nothing to do with the argument that I have been suggesting – except as another illustration of the strength of the Subject/Object dichotomy within our tradition of reasonable enquiry. My experience is rooted in my language which is never mine but always ours. Even as I have what I take to be a most private thought or most personal experience, I exemplify my membership of the language-community in which such understandings arise and my commitment to the mode of existence which sustains it. My community is always present in my speech, because, in representing objects, it re-presents a way of knowledge.

Of course, it is entirely possible for me to see 'differently'; for instance, to react to what everybody takes to be a command as if it were an endearment or greeting. But to respond in this way is to be taken to be playing an unknown game. If our known games constitute our society, to seem to play an unknown game is to be seen to propose an unknown society – hence, perhaps, to be recognizably 'mad'. So we come to the following 'description' of 'madness': to be 'mad' is to be seen to engage in activities which appear to propose an unknown society. Yet even my very act of seeing things 'differently' from my fellows is only recognized as 'different' through the common language which we share. Once again, this common language *is* the way in which we live our lives together. So the claim to 'difference' and its recognition – whether as madman or genius – re-presents the sameness and unity of the mode of existence of our community.

Notice how, like all descriptions, my 'description' of 'madness' constitutes its phenomenon. Like all speech, it relies on and sustains a persuasive version of a possible society. Yet to be 'persuaded' is to come to accept that its speech represents a recognizable object. Alternatively, we may hear speech as re-presenting our way of knowledge. In this listening mode, we are concerned neither with persuading nor with being persuaded, but with making ourself open to what is always already there within our speech – our-selves, our community.

If speech is always a token of our commitment to some possible society, to be a member of a society is to play its language-games.

To understand a society is to speak its language and so to 'see', 'look', and 'listen', 'properly'. As he looks back on his conversations with don Juan, Castaneda comes close to making the same point:

> To any beginner, Indian or non-Indian, the knowledge of sorcery was rendered incomprehensible by the outlandish characteristics of the phenomena he experienced. Personally, as a Western man, I found these characteristics so bizarre that it was virtually impossible to explain them in terms of my own everyday life, and I was forced to the conclusion that any attempt to classify my field data in my own terms would be futile.
>
> Thus it became obvious to me that don Juan's knowledge had to be examined in terms of how he himself understood it; only in such terms could it be made evident and convincing. (pp. 19-20)

For Castaneda, to explain don Juan's knowledge in terms of a Western system of classification was pointless ('any attempt to classify my field data in my own terms would be futile'). For it would constitute it as a feature of Western knowledge, but not of don Juan's knowledge. Only in don Juan's terms could the Yaqui version of sorcery be properly apprehended.

Yet notice how Castaneda cannot shake off the 'picture theory' of language. While re-membering that a way of knowledge constitutes its objects, he still writes of the 'outlandish' and 'bizarre' characteristics of 'phenomena' and of 'field data' *as if they await explication* through a way of knowledge. Yet the experience of phenomena and the recognition of field data is the *guarantee that the world has already been explicated* through a way of knowledge. So it is not as if we have experiences and then try to understand them. Our experience is our understanding. Our understanding is our commitment to a persuasive version of a possible society.

So Castaneda's path is long and difficult. The acceptance of description as representation, of language as a mirror, *is* the persuasive version which sustains our society. It is our society's language for talking about itself. Scientific explanations, works of art, everyday accounts, are all persuasive because, in understanding them as they wish to be understood, we sustain our communal mode of existence.

Re-member the appeal of 'realism' in the novel, cinema, or theatre. 'Realism' demands not simply that the 'events' depicted should be 'true-to-life', but, more crucially, that art should not question the convention that speech 'represents by words'. And this is always more than a convention: it re-presents the manner in which our society apprehends itself, is itself:

> For a particular society, in fact, the work that is realistic is that which represents the perceived forms of 'Reality'. It is a question of reiterating the society's system of intelligibility. (Heath, 1972, p. 21)

As Heath puts it, in writing 'realistically', whether as novelists, scientists or bureaucrats, we 'reiterate' our 'society's system of intelligibility'. Notice that this applies equally to works which openly support the *status quo* or are critical in intent. For criticism which 'respects the perceived forms of "Reality" ' sustains what it criticizes. In this sense, criticism (which fails to listen to its own language) is acceptance (of speech as representation, of our mode of existence).

In the course of this discussion of 'description', we have distinguished description as 'representation' from description as 're-presentation'. Yet, lest we feel that we have, in this way, exerted our authority over language, or captured the character of the world, we should re-member that any such distinction never settles the matter but provides another occasion for thinking. For language and world are never fully 'objects' of our reflection. Rather than 'capture' language, we participate, as persons, in and through it. Yet neither are we captured *by* language. Language is not a prison which prevents me from saying my say, any more than it prevents Castaneda from gathering 'field data'. Rather, in speaking, we express our-selves through the commitment which our speech exemplifies to a tradition of enquiry which proposes a possible society.

Suggestions for further reading

As I suggested in the course of this chapter, a great deal of the version of 'description' which it proposes, is drawn from my reading of the work of the philosopher, Ludwig Wittgenstein.

J. L. Austin's *Sense and Sensibilia* (1962) is an ordinary-language account of 'reality', while Wittgenstein's own writings can be approached through *Philosophical Investigations* (1969 edition) and *On Certainty* (1970 edition). Hanna Pitkin's superb *Wittgenstein and Justice* (1972) is by far the best assessment of the importance of his work for the social sciences. It has the added attraction of assuming little or no background knowledge of either.

Semiology, or the science of signs, has also been an important area for the discussion of description. The work of Saussure, its founder, is best presented (and critiqued) in the work of Roland Barthes. I especially recommend Barthes, *Writing Degree Zero* (1967).

The notions of 'listening to' and 'hearing' language, which are introduced towards the end of the chapter, I take from the contemporary German philosopher, Martin Heidegger. Since his work makes difficult reading for the non-specialist, I would suggest a series of books which are particularly concerned with his implications for the social sciences. These include Alan Blum, *Theorizing* (1974); P. McHugh *et al.*, *On the Beginning of Social Inquiry* (1974); P. Filmer *et al.* (forthcoming), *Stratifying Practices: Essays in Reflexive Sociology*, which includes a paper of mine ('Davis and Moore, market speech and community'); and David Silverman and Jill Jones, *Organizational Work: The Language of Grading, the Grading of Language* (1975).

3
Method/Rule

Method – An orderly procedure or process; hence a set form of procedures, as in investigation or instruction . . . (*Webster's Collegiate Dictionary*, fifth edition)
Rule – Principle to which action or procedure conforms or is bound or intended to conform . . . (*Concise Oxford Dictionary*, fifth edition)

Castaneda's search for understanding seems always to turn on a search for methods and rules. His questioning of don Juan continually revolves around the 'set form of procedures', the 'principle to which action or procedure conforms or is bound or intended to conform', through which, he believes, don Juan makes sense of non-ordinary reality. Notice Castaneda's comment about don Juan's suggestion that he should find a 'spot' on the floor where he could sit without fatigue:

> What he had posed as a problem to be solved was certainly a riddle. I had no idea how to begin or even what he had in mind. Several times I asked for a clue, or at least a hint, as to how to proceed in locating a point where I felt happy and strong. I insisted and argued that I had no idea what he really meant because I couldn't conceive the problem. (p. 31)

Castaneda feels he cannot 'conceive the problem' without knowing the methods he must employ and the rules he must follow. He therefore wants 'a clue, or at least a hint, as to how to proceed'. Given information about 'how to proceed', given methods and rules, it might be possible to understand the elements of don Juan's way of knowledge, perhaps even to see as he sees – to see 'what he really meant'.

Now don Juan is sometimes far more forthcoming about his 'methods' than he seems to be during the 'spot' episode. Indeed, many pages of Castaneda's book report highly intricate instructions from don Juan on the preparation of hallucinogenic materials and on the settings in which they should properly be taken; for instance, in the case of the preparation of *datura* paste and the role of the lizards when using it, Castaneda cannot complain of lack of guidance on methods. Yet so much of don Juan's instructions are concerned entirely with technique rather than with the character of the experiences that may follow. For instance, on a trip to Chihuahua to gather mushrooms for peyote, Castaneda tries to get don Juan talking about Mescalito, the protector and teacher whom one encounters through peyote:

> He seemed to be very annoyed by my questioning. I told him I had to ask all these questions because I wanted to find out all I could.
> 'Don't ask *me!*' He smiled maliciously. 'Ask *him*. The next time you see him, ask him everything you want to know.'
> 'Then Mescalito *is* like a person you can talk . . .'
> He did not let me finish. He turned away, picked up the canteen, stepped down from the ledge, and disappeared around the rock. (p. 93)

Don Juan's comments seem to suggest the crazy double-bind that Joseph Heller proposes in his novel, *Catch-22*. To get out of the army and be sent home, you have to be declared insane but, in such a situation, to ask to be declared insane is obviously a sane act, therefore people who seek to be declared insane must be sane. Only crazy people would not ask to be declared insane. Similarly, Castaneda's attempts to find out how he might recognize Mescalito are greeted by the response: 'Don't ask *me!* Ask *him*.' But how is Castaneda going to 'ask him' when he needs such information *prior* to encountering Mescalito? So 'asking him' is doubly irrelevant to Castaneda's plight: either he will not

know how to recognize Mescalito and so will not be able to ask
him, or, by recognizing him, he will have found out what he
needs to know already and so will not have to ask.

Not only will don Juan not reveal what is *to be* experienced,
he usually will not accept what Castaneda takes to be the most
obvious features of what *has been* experienced, as he recounts it
to don Juan. For instance, when Castaneda takes peyote for the
first time, he tells don Juan afterwards that he experienced great
fear. But don Juan says:

> 'You are not thinking in the proper order. Mescalito actually
> played with you. That's the point to think about. Why don't
> you dwell on that instead of on your fear?' (p. 51)

Later Castaneda tells don Juan that he's not sure whether he
really had a certain experience or whether he had 'thought it up'.
Was he really a crow? Don Juan politely reprimands him for
asking such a question:

> 'Don't think about whether you remembered it or made it up.
> Such thoughts fit men only. They do not fit crows.' (p. 169)

For don Juan, it seems, clearly Castaneda's methods are mistaken. 'You are not thinking in the proper order,' he tells him.
And again: 'Don't think about whether you remembered it or
made it up.' Instead, Castaneda should have concentrated on the
fact that 'Mescalito actually played with' him and, later, should
have thought as a crow thinks. Yet these alternative rules for
making sense never seem to be revealed prior to an experience.
On the contrary, they are continually introduced as ways of
contradicting the accounts of his experiences that Castaneda
offers after the event. Further, each 'rule' trades off the double-
bind to which I have been alluding. What can it mean to con-
centrate on Mescalito's 'playing' with you or to think as a 'crow'?
To know the answer means that you do not need don Juan's
advice. Not to know the answer is likely to mean that any rules
that don Juan might offer will turn out to be incomprehensible.

Given Castaneda's apparent repeated incomprehension, perhaps
the source of his difficulty is neither his stupidity nor don Juan's
arrogance. Perhaps his (our) incomprehension presents an occasion
to re-member our notions of 'method' and 'rule'? We conceive of

D

methods and rules as organized means ('an orderly procedure or process', a 'principle') to achieve specified ends ('investigation', 'instruction'). Deep within our understanding of them is a conception of 'method' and 'rule' as 'technique', as the instrument we employ in order to achieve our ends. To follow methods is to be organized, to be method-ical. So our emphasis on technique, on 'how to do it', allows us to recognize that there are always rules anyone can follow to produce whatever outcome we desire (a 'good' experience, a highly-regarded essay, etc.). If we don't happen to know the rules, we can always turn to one of the many books of instructions. If no such book has been written in relation to a particular desired outcome, then we can at least plan our activities, and so think about our methods beforehand. Of course, seeking and following proper methods and rules need not mean that the desired outcome will always be attained. The circumstances may work against us (we may not have the ability or the resources), or we may fail to apply the rules in the 'proper' way. Yet follow rules we must if we are to hope to attain any-thing worth while. Otherwise, we label our-selves disorganized, haphazard and un-methodical.

Yet this conception of methods and rules as techniques which are both essential and always at our service does not seem to be recognized in the ways in which don Juan speaks to Castaneda. For instance, in discussing the devil's weed, don Juan mentions that it will teach you 'unimaginable things':

> 'Like what, don Juan?'
> 'That I can't tell you. Every man is different. My benefactor never told me what he had learned. He told me how to proceed, but never what he saw. That is only for oneself.'
> 'But I tell you all I see, don Juan.'
> 'Now you do. Later you will not.' (p. 127)

For don Juan, it seems, the uniqueness of personal experience is precious ('Every man is different'). To learn a technique by which to recognize 'unimaginable things' is to negate the unique 'seeing' which is every man's expression of himself. For technique (methods, rules as we conceive them), by specifying discrete paths to knowledge, closes off other paths and diverts our attention away from those experiences which, because they seem personally valid for (as) us, seem to transcend technique. Compare for instance the 'suggestions' of sex manuals with the experience of the sexual act. Where we find the former failing, it is not so much that the techniques are inadequate or in insufficient detail but that we sense a deep separation between any technique and the experience. To 'employ' their techniques can be to lose sight of the immediate validity of our experience for us, here and now. Indeed, we may grasp that, rather than our 'employing' the techniques, the techniques are 'employing' us. The technique is no longer at our service, rather we are at 'its' service. In this way I read the sense of don Juan's reference to his benefactor's teaching: 'He told me how to proceed, but never what he saw. That is only for oneself.' While it is churlish to refuse to offer advice about the practical circumstances which set the background for an experience ('He told me how to proceed'), the experience itself is only concealed by technique ('That is only for oneself').

It follows from our identification of method with being methodical, that we are always seeking to formulate methods and rules in abstraction from particular circumstances. Then, we feel, if we knew this general method (this 'orderly procedure', this 'principle'), we can apply it to whatever situation confronts us, as the need arises. Yet don Juan rarely talks 'abstractly' or about 'orderly procedures' or 'principles'. Nearly all his discussions of the character of Castaneda's experiences occur *after* particular events. He always requires a long account from Castaneda of his latest experiences before he will offer any comment. He stresses to Castaneda that it is particularly important to get an account of the order in which 'things' happened to him. What don Juan then will say will always make sense only in terms of that event as recognized by (constituted in) the talk of the two parties.

So, as don Juan maintains, without knowing the occasion and the instance to which one is referring, making sense of experience is a worthless exercise. While we are used to talking 'abstractly' about rules and principles, for don Juan the interpretation and application of a rule is always an entirely *practical* matter, related to concrete occasions at which we try to make sense of an activity for the purposes which are relevant at the time. So rules come to be intelligible in, and through, the experience (or the invention) of instances to which they might be applicable and the negotiation of a 'proper' application of the rule, in the light of all the circumstances. Any 'abstract' list of rules (or methods) only makes sense, then, with reference to concrete or hypothetical instances. Appearing to talk abstractly about rules, as for instance, when preparing new rules of committee procedure, is only brought off by glossing over this activity.

Yet our common ability to generate and recognize 'proper' instances is a guarantee that, while our experiences can be both unique and valid for us, the way of knowledge that any understanding affirms cannot be ours alone. Consider this exchange between Castaneda and don Juan after Castaneda has had his first experience with peyote:

> 'In what way does my experience differ from that of others?'
> 'You're not an Indian; therefore it is hard for me to figure out what is what.' (p. 45)

I take the force of don Juan's remark 'You're not an Indian', to reside in an assertion that the Indian way of recognizing experiences is fundamentally different from the Western way. As I argued in the previous chapter, communally-sanctioned recognitions of 'experiences' *constitute* the experiences (for members of the community). Of course, this does not deny that different Indians, just as much as different Western men, can have different experiences. However, that 'difference' is itself grounded within the community that the experience re-members. So, as I read a sense of don Juan's remark, we only come to 'see' 'differences' and 'instances' by invoking a way of knowledge that already provides how each may be properly accounted. Each man is, indeed, unique for don Juan, but the uniqueness of his experience is only available to him (and to us) in and through the community which his speech re-collects.

It follows that the double-bind, to which I referred earlier, is inherent in any understanding, for that understanding can only express what, in a deep sense, one knows already. Examine don Juan's responses to Castaneda's questions about his experience with the 'little smoke':

> 'Did you behave the same way I did when you smoked for the first time, don Juan?'

'No, it wasn't the same. We have different characters.'

'How did you behave?'

Don Juan did not answer. I rephrased the question and asked it again. But he said he did not remember his experiences, and that my question was comparable to asking a fisherman how he felt the first time he fished. (p. 138)

Here, once again, there is the stress on the validity of each man's experience for himself ('No it [my experience] wasn't the same. We have different characters'). Yet, in his next response, Castaneda reports that don Juan compared his question to 'asking a fisherman how he felt the first time he fished'. There is no explanation in the text as to what don Juan may have intended by this remark. The way I read the analogy between questioning a *brujo* and questioning a fisherman is that, in both cases, to understand 'properly' a reply to a question it is necessary already to grasp (and be grasped by) the way of knowledge of the community concerned. For a 'proper' understanding can only be an understanding that is warranted by that community's persuasive version of the world. Methods and rules no longer present themselves as isolated 'techniques' to be used, as necessary, by an isolated person concerned with his private ends. Instead, in acting as in-accord-with-a-rule, in recognizing the methodic character of an activity, we collect our-selves into a community which always pre-figures any rule and any method. There are no independent methods and rules which communities may choose to employ. Rather, the method and the rule *is* the community.

In using our methods and rules, we get a sense of exerting mastery over a technique. We feel that we are using this technique for our purposes. Yet this occurs in forgetfulness of the community that the application of a rule in a 'proper' context necessarily re-collects. So, in applying techniques, we become forgetful of the claim to community which is always present in our speech. Which is to say, we fail to re-member our-selves. In exerting mastery over technique, we are mastered by technique; in using it, it uses us. Still better, it becomes us – we are technique.

This rejection of the selves which our activities collect is precisely what is required from users of techniques. They are to be mere operatives, faceless men, interchangeable with other faceless men, applying technique without bias, without fear or favour. And this is doubly forgetful. For to read Castaneda's questions is to be struck by an absence. An absence of the self which his questions express and re-member. His questions could be the questions of any-man, just as the routine scientific paper presents itself as any-scientist's text. Such texts are forgetful of the self that any activity collects by its call to (and upon) a community and a particular- historical epoch. They forget, further, that understanding is never passive. It is always Me, here, now, *producing* sense – as I produce sense by my reading of Castaneda's text. So my writing and reading are always acts of production – of possible societies, of selves. And that production is both mine and not mine alone. Mine because in my acts of production I re-member my-self. Not mine alone because 'I' exist in and through a dialogue with a tradition that always already precedes me, and with an emerging social order that will be the readings of my text.

Indexical and objective expressions

In order to advance my argument about the character of method and rule, I am going to have to make a distinction which, while familiar to philosophers, linguists and some sociologists, is by no means part of everyday speech. It is the distinction between 'indexical' and 'objective' expressions.

An 'indexical' expression is some activity (a statement, a glance, a gesture, etc.) that we treat as an index of an underlying reality. For instance, an indexical statement points towards something (an underlying reality) which we can discover by knowing or assuming things about the purposes of the speaker, the occasion on which his statement is uttered and the previous and potential course of the interaction during which it was expressed. In other words, we can make sense of indexical statements by locating a 'proper' context for them. For instance:

*'Hello', or *'I am a crow'.†

Both statements only come to make sense by locating a 'proper' context. Even though 'Hello' immediately strikes one as sane talk

† Henceforth, asterisks will denote hypothetical statements.

and 'I am a crow' as crazy talk, such matters are only settled on
the occasions at which such utterances are heard. For example, if
'Hello' were to be heard from a person half-way through an on-
going conversation, then it might strike the others as bizarre. It
couldn't possibly be a greeting because greetings are only offered
at the outset of conversations – we might say that greetings 'do'
the beginning of a conversation. Said in this context, then, 'Hello'
can only be a joke or a threat or what? So we search for further
clues. Conversely 'I am a crow' might make perfectly proper
and obvious sense when, say, tied to an announcement by a
mime-artist about his next (or present) performance. Equally, in
giving these examples and relying upon you to read some sense
into them, I am drawing upon our common competence to
'remedy' the unspoken part by adding an intelligible context. So
I don't have to concoct the utterance:

*'Having entered the room, I want to greet you, so "Hello".'

You are already able to recognize 'Hello', in most circumstances,
as a greeting, without my having to spell out a form of words
that points this out. Indeed, such 'spelling out' is positively dis-
ruptive of everyday conversation, where routinely repeated words
and phrases serve quite well to index underlying meanings – for
all practical purposes. Imagine how my longer version of 'Hello'
might be received in an everyday setting.

An 'objective' expression, on the other hand, is an activity
that makes sense in itself, without our having to locate a context
which provides the underlying reality that an 'indexical' expression
indexes. So an 'objective' statement is a statement which claims
to tell us about 'things' ('real' or 'imaginary'), without our having
to locate a context to make sense of its description or explanation.
Consider Castaneda's questions:

'Then Mescalito is real?' (p. 45)
'Did I really fly?' (p. 128)
'Did I really become a crow?' (p. 172)

All ask to be told what was really happening at the time. All
require an objective statement in reply. So the force of 'real-ly'
in the three questions is the attempt to discover a context-free
sense of what was going on. A sense which would be separate

from both the occasion on which the question is posed (e.g. a scientific meeting; a discussion between a *brujo* and his apprentice; gossip) and the occasion at which the experiences in question occurred (during a dream, under drugs, during a routine activity).

The relevance of this distinction to my discussion of method is two-fold.

1 Many of our activities rely upon our ability to distinguish and move backwards and forwards between indexical and objective expressions.

2 The means of distinguishing and moving between the two is what I want to re-present as method or rule.

Such a view of method seems to be expressed in the writings of the classical French sociologist, Émile Durkheim. In his *Rules of Sociological Method* (1895), Durkheim argues that, if sociology is to escape crude subjectivism, it must concern itself with a body of facts that both stand outside individual consciousness and constrain it. These facts Durkheim will call *social* facts:

> every way of acting which is general throughout a given society, while at the same time existing in its own right independent of its individual manifestations. (1964, p. 13)

Notice Durkheim's stress on the 'generality' of social facts and their existence 'in their own right'. For Durkheim, then, social facts are, in themselves, objective – they are 'the way things are'. Unlike consciousness and perception, which always require a context, social facts exist in the realm of solid objectivity, quite outside human subjectivity. Moreover, for Durkheim, since subjectivity can only be studied subjectively, the objectivity of social facts is the grounding basis for an objective social science. As he writes:

> In order to follow a methodical course, we must establish the foundations of science on solid ground and not on shifting sand. We must approach the social realm where it offers the easiest access to scientific investigation. (*ibid.*, p. 46)

Notice how Durkheim grounds his notion of social science on being method-ical ('follow[ing] a methodical course'). It is to be method which dictates what is to be studied ('solid ground') and what is to be avoided ('shifting sand'). Only the former offers 'the easiest access to scientific investigation'.

So, for Durkheim, one becomes scientific by becoming method-ical. To be method-ical one must only select objective expressions for study – so, for instance, Durkheim will make a great deal of official statistics, social facts which, for him, are free from indexicality. Finally, to be method-ical, one must follow rules which ensure that one's scientific account, in turn, is an objective expression. And, in a chapter entitled 'Rules for the observation of social facts', Durkheim will tell us what these rules are. The method-ical researcher must consider social facts 'as things', for:

> To treat phenomena as things is to treat them as data, and these constitute the point of departure for science. (*ibid.*, p. 27)

To consider social facts as 'data', we must define the group of phenomena that concern us in advance of our study. Further, such definitions must be in terms of certain common characteristics of the data. We must assess the facts as a whole, concentrating on common external features and ignoring individual manifestations. Above all, advises Durkheim, we must eradicate all our preconceptions.

Durkheim implies that, having followed such rules, we can produce objective accounts: accounts which correspond to the way things are rather than to our preconceptions of their nature. And this claim to correspondence is to be based on our appeal to method and to rule. An appeal which defines for us our topics ('social facts', 'the point of departure for science') and the manner in which we shall investigate them (by the 'eradication of all our preconceptions'). For Durkheim, then, the account that is most fully an 'objective expression' is, in every sense, impersonal. Through our focus on 'proper' data, through our use of 'proper' methods, such an account will stand as an authentic report on the way things are. Untouched by human hands, our account will be the very voice of Nature relaying its own message about itself.

Durkheim's insistence on the need for a scientific status for our accounts and his emphasis that such a status can only be accorded to objective accounts, guaranteed by adherence to the scientific method, expresses the common concerns of the scientific community. Above all else, that community sustains its difference (its 'expertness') by its avoidance of indexical expressions and by its insistence on an analysis of its 'data'; from, what Durkheim

calls, 'an aspect that is independent of their individual manifestations'. The further one is away from individual facts, forever
locked into unrecoverable contexts, the closer to 'objective
expressions' our accounts can become. As Durkheim puts it:

> We may lay down as a principle that social facts lend themselves
> more readily to objective representation in proportion as their
> separation from the individual facts expressing them is more
> complete. (*ibid.*, p. 44)

So the ideal is an 'objective representation' of a 'social fact', an
'objective expression' of an 'objective expression'. And here
Durkheim is in accord with the claim to authority on which
scientific work grounds itself. Such a claim provides that, while
context can never be neglected, objective statements are necessary
for exactness. Indeed, the distinction between 'objective' and
'indexical' expressions constitutes that between 'science' and
'hearsay', and grounds the scientific community's claim to expertness. Given the insistence upon a need for 'objective' expressions,
where context does enter into a scientific account, it is seen to
arise from practical difficulties (e.g. 'unclear' propositions, 'ill-
defined' terms) which can be remedied. Such remedies (testing,
use of operational definitions) resolve the practical difficulties and
lead to the replacement of a context-bound statement with an
'objective representation'. Science calls these remedies for indexicality 'methods' and refers to the logic of methods as 'methodology'.

But the reliance on 'method' as a claim to authority is not
restricted to the scientific community. Consider the following
extract from a set of notes prepared by a personnel department
for the guidance of staff about to undergo assessments of their
'career potential':

> The assessment of potential depends a great deal on intuitive
> judgment based on fact and must clearly be as objective as
> possible. We hope to achieve this by bringing into the dis-
> cussion a number of people, the majority of whom know
> something of the individual being discussed. (Taken from
> research materials discussed in Silverman and Jones, 1975)

The aim stated here is the production of a non-indexical account –
an account that is 'as objective as possible'. This is to be sought

by using only facts as data ('intuitive judgment based on fact') and by using the familiarity of the assessors with the candidates as a remedy for indexicality. While context is always important, it can be recognized and controlled – after all, 'the majority of [the assessors] . . . know something of the individual'. So to be serious, in terms of this note, is to be 'objective'. To be 'objective' is to be method-ical. Being a 'proper' bureaucrat, just as much as being a 'proper' scientist, means showing one's commitments to the 'facts' and to the correct methods whereby the facts may be assessed. So the bureaucrat must act in what the German sociologist Max Weber has called 'a spirit of formalistic impersonality'. His actions are never allowed to be viewed merely as 'his' but as the actions of an 'official' holding an 'office' and following rules. He is to be seen as simply the instrument of the rule-book. His undisputed claim to authority is always: 'I may not like doing this but I'm only doing my job (going by the book, etc.).' He always provides that he shall be seen to be acting 'impersonally', under the auspices of the 'proper' rule.

Given the similarity of the scientific and bureaucratic claims to authority (what I have taken to be their claim to be taken seriously), and the dominance of scientific and bureaucratic modes of under- standing within our society, it is hardly surprising that adherence to method and rule are often taken as standards of seriousness in everyday discourse. We rely frequently on being able to move from hearsay, from 'subjective' interpretations, to the 'facts' of the matter. And like expert communities, we feel we are able to move from the former to the latter by the adoption of methods and rules. For instance, when Castaneda, while using the 'little smoke', experiences a feeling that his head is going through a pole, he writes that:

> In a desperate search for a rational explanation I concluded that my eyes were distorting depth, and that the pole must have been ten feet away, even though I saw it directly in front of my face. I then conceived a logical, rational way to check the position of the pole. (p. 134)

Notice how Castaneda will not trust his experience and must search for an objective account of 'the way things are' ('In a desperate search for a rational explanation'). The aim, for him, is always to be rational. His fear, discussed in an earlier chapter, is that of 'losing all my rationality'. To be 'rational' is to be 'logical' – look at how these words are used almost synonymously by Castaneda ('I then conceived a logical, rational way'). To be logical is to be (governed by) technique – to consider a 'way to *check* the position of the pole'. So the sense of Castaneda's 'logical, rational way' (to check the position of the pole) arises for me in the conviction that methods (expressed in such techniques as testing) arbitrate between mere 'opinions' and establish 'facts'. Like the accounts of scientists and bureaucrats, Castaneda's 'conclusion' demands to be taken seriously because of its concern to move from an 'indexical' to an 'objective' statement and its demonstration that method is to be the mechanism of such movement.

The success of method

Do methods succeed? They seem to. Like Castaneda, we can usually tell an opinion from a fact and, when in doubt, know how to 'check'. But how do methods succeed? Or, to put the question in another way: what do rules and methods do for us and what do we do with them?

Let us consider an example. Say a visitor from another culture wanted to write a letter. While speaking English, he was unfamiliar with letter-writing in general and the composition of 'correct' letters in this country. He asks for your advice and, being a method-ical kind of person, you offer to draw him up a list of rules which, if he follows them, will enable him to write letters 'correctly'. Then imagine the visitor writing a letter under the guidance of these rules. Say it occurred to him that he wanted to say more after he had signed his name. He then approaches you and says:

* 'You told me how my letters must end. As I now wish to write more, I had better tear up this letter and write another one.'

You reply that there is no need to tear up the letter. It is quite in order to make additions to a letter after one has signed. By writing P.S. after his signature and adding his additional message after that, all will be well.

The visitor now enquires whether it is always all right to add a post-script to a letter. You reply:

* 'It's generally all right but it's not usually done when writing a formal or business letter.'

The visitor thanks you but now looks at you a little quizzically. Since letter-writing now seems to be rather more complicated than he had originally been led to understand, and so that he will be able to write letters when you are not available to offer advice, he requests you to write a *new* set of rules. This new set will contain instructions about how to *apply* the first set, i.e. the kinds of occasions on which the rules must be followed entirely, can be modified or can be disregarded.

I think you would now be in something of a fix. You could accede to his request but that would be no guarantee that he would not come back to you once more needing a third set of rules – rules for the application of rules for the application of rules – and so on. Alternatively, you could reply:

* 'Well all this is really common sense.'

But, once again, he could always come back to you with a remark like:

* 'Well, I agree. But your common sense is not my common sense. Please list your rules of common sense.'

At this point, no doubt, the friendship would be at an end!

The letter-writing example, and there are innumerable others (crossing a road, buying goods at a shop, paying your fare on a bus, and so on), suggests that, by themselves, rules cannot cover every instance that we might come to recognize. We employ rules (and use methods) and seem to be constrained by them because as common-sense people, we can tell when it makes sense to invoke a particular rule and in what spirit. So, as members, rules and methods do not, in themselves, govern what we do. Rather, they are the means through which we recognize the orderly character of others' behaviour and provide for the orderly character of our own. And to apply a rule is our election of the sense of the world which, like a self-fulfilling prophecy, constitutes the

character of that which it addresses. Consider Durkheim's
comment about the status of his 'social facts':

> To treat the facts of a certain order as things is not, then, to place
> them in a certain category of reality but to assume a *certain
> mental attitude* toward them on the principle that when approach-
> ing their study we are absolutely ignorant of their nature, and
> that their characteristic properties, like the unknown causes on
> which they depend, cannot be discovered by even the most
> careful introspection. (*op. cit.*, p. xliii, emphasis mine)

Durkheim re-asserts, in this passage, the objective character of
social facts ('the facts of a certain order') and emphasizes that it
is only by empirical study that we can grasp 'their characteristic
properties'. 'Even the most careful introspection', he writes, is
quite inadequate compared to scientific research. But notice how
Durkheim concedes that social facts have to be addressed in the
proper manner *before* we can study them. Social facts only become
available for study if we 'assume a certain mental attitude toward
them'. So Durkheim's whole enterprise only becomes possible if
we elect to follow his methods for addressing the social world.
Because such methods are not simply means of studying the
world, but constitute the world's character for purposes of study
(in Durkheim's case as a 'social fact'), they no longer seem like
techniques to be used instrumentally for an observer's ends.

In writing this way, Durkheim seems to be trying to side-step
the metaphysical debate about the 'real' character of reality. To
consider social facts as 'things', he affirms, is 'not . . . to place
them in a certain category of reality'; it is merely, for scientific
purposes, 'to assume a certain mental attitude toward them'. But
his side-step from metaphysics is only from one metaphysical
position to another. For, if social facts are not 'a certain category
of reality' but merely what we see when we 'assume a certain
mental attitude', then Durkheim seems to be taking a stand firmly
in a subjectivist position. Yet, whether social facts are, to use the
phrases of the previous chapter, 'the way things are' or, merely,
'the way we see things', this passage confirms that we constitute
what our words address in and through our words. So method
no longer seems like a technique *brought* to speech; it is always
within our speech, within the way of knowledge which the speech

elects and proposes. Hence, in discussing social facts, Durkheim's text does not 'assume a certain mental attitude *toward them*' because social facts only exist in and through the system of intelligibility which his text affirms. He merely 'assumes a certain mental attitude'. Thereby, he finds self as a functionary of the scientific community.

What methods – viewed as technique – do for us, then, is to affirm our claim to membership of bureaucratic/scientific communities with technical purposes. Methods use us; for, in writing under the auspices of 'correct method', we find ourselves as faceless men, producing accounts which can only be taken seriously by denying our presence within them. The ideal is to be 'untouched by human hands'.

Yet what we do with methods, all the time denies this nonhuman character that we want to claim for our speech. As the letter-writing example suggests, whenever an 'objective expression' is offered, supposedly governed by a set of rules which any man could follow, something is forgotten. The rule, in itself, cannot produce a 'proper' outcome. We must already know what a 'proper' invocation of a rule looks like; we must already understand the 'spirit' of the rule and be able to identify 'proper' instances to which it can be applied. So the sense of any outcome, of any speech, rests upon a body of unformulated common-sense practices used to recognize contexts and to apply rules 'in the right spirit'. And these practices reflect (are) our membership of society.

Durkheim's classic study called *Suicide* (1952), illustrates our common ability, as members, to make sense of outcomes – in this case, the recognition and explanation of acts of 'suicide'. Durkheim addresses suicide as a social fact expressed in official statistics giving the rate of mortality through suicide for different societies. He insists that he is not concerned with the individual manifestations of the act, nor with the suicidal (or other) intentions of the deceased. For, following his injunctions in *The Rules of Sociological Method*, the further one distances one's investigation from individual cases and from subjective states of mind, the more 'social facts lend themselves . . . to objective representation'.

So, for Durkheim, suicide has a factual character: suicide exists separately from how we conceive it at any particular time. As a consequence, he rejects common-sense notions of suicide in favour of a more objective definition. Objects must be explained objectively. It follows that common-sense usages of the term must be supplanted by a scientific definition which accords with the order of facts that 'suicide' represents. Durkheim puts it this way:

> Our first task, then, must be to determine the order of facts to be studied under the name of suicides. Accordingly, we must enquire, whether, among the different varieties of death, some have common qualities, objective enough to be recognizable *by all honest observers*. (1952, p. 42, emphasis mine)

This passage suggests that, for Durkheim, there is a distinction between the organization of the social world (in this case, 'the different varieties of death') and 'studies' and 'enquiries' as to its nature. Certainly, objective studies will correspond to that world but they will only do so through the adoption of correct methods. So 'the order of facts' does not speak for itself. If it is to be studied properly it must be recognized correctly. And the method for correct recognition of 'the order of facts' is to rely on what is 'objective enough to be recognizable by all honest observers'.

Now, of course, 'honest observers' can and will agree about abstract definitions of terms. After all, dictionaries do get compiled. But how does a dictionary get compiled? And how do the 'objective qualities' recognized by 'all honest observers' relate to actual cases? We can make definitions and understand them because we are always already members of some society. We can apply a set of qualities and recognize the good sense of any particular application for the same reason. All enquiry, all understanding, is always located within membership. So to enquire about a particular aspect of membership – in this case, the 'order of facts' which 'suicide' represents – is to guarantee that one asks questions and understands answers always, necessarily, as a member.

Given our membership, we can, in our everyday activities, recognize a state of affairs as necessarily a 'suicide', without needing to refer to or to develop an abstract definition of the term. Equally, as scientists, we are able to see why a particular instance does, or does not, accord with our operational definition of 'suicide'. In both cases, whether we understand the facts of the matter as coroners or scientists, we express our membership in our ability to detect a rule-governed body of facts. So, as members, we know in countless ways, on countless occasions, that rules cannot cover every possible instance and must always contain '*et cetera* clauses'. Such extensions to the rules allow us to apply rules properly to occasions when it seems reasonable to do so, even if such occasions are not specifically mentioned in the rules. We know that it can sometimes be correct to contravene a rule, when such a contravention would make sense as in-the-spirit-of-the-rule. Contraventions like this, we greet with 'let it pass'. We know further that the sense of an event (a statement, a gesture) may not be immediately obvious and that we must be prepared to 'wait and see'. So we generally take the sense of something to be determined by what happens subsequently. We don't jump to conclusions before seeing how an activity unfolds. We also know that outcomes always have causes. So, given any recognizable outcome, we know (or seek to find out) why it must have happened that way – even where we had thought originally that it might not turn out that way. Above all, we know that questions and courses of enquiry are directed towards what might be required 'for all practical purposes'. So they always begin by ruling out what it would be foolish (time-wasting, irrelevant) to enquire into, and conclude at a point where 'sufficient' is known 'for all practical purposes'.

Such practices are unavoidably involved in recognizing actual cases (of 'suicide'). However clear our notion of the nature of the phenomenon in question, that notion does not apply itself. As I am observed to open a medicine cupboard, take out and swallow a quantity of pills, as a note is found by my body, the case must be recognized as 'for all practical purposes', 'letting pass' all contrary information; what we now see 'must have been' a case of 'suicide' – although further information might make us change our mind.

The philosopher Ludwig Wittgenstein came to much this conclusion about the importance of recognizing instances, when he considered the rules of mathematics. Say we are trying to follow the rules of calculation, he suggests, how do we know that we are following the rules *in the right way*? Are there circumstances or conditions which ensure the correct employment of rules?:

E

But can it be seen from a *rule* what circumstances logically
exclude a mistake in the employment of rules of calculation?
What use is a rule to us here? Mightn't we (in turn) go wrong
in applying it? (1970 edition, para. 26)

In opening up the possibility of rules for rules of application
('Mightn't we (in turn) go wrong in applying [the rule]?'),
Wittgenstein is circling around the same problem as I raised in
the letter-writing example. The search for all-encompassing rules
is endless and never successful. We only end it by practical considerations ('getting on with things'), when dealing with particular
instances.

Wittgenstein goes on:

If, however, one wanted to give something like a rule here,
then it would contain the expression 'in normal circumstances'.
And we recognize normal circumstances but cannot precisely describe them. At most, we can describe a range of abnormal ones.
What is 'learning a rule'? – *This*.
What is 'making a mistake in applying it'? – *This*. And what
is pointed to here is something indeterminate. (*ibid.*, paras 27-8)

Wittgenstein is saying that we have to point to instances ('*This*')
when talking about rules and rule-following. Our ability to talk
abstractly about rules, or, without reflection, to be able to follow
a rule, lies on our competence to recognize 'normal circumstances'
without being able ever to formulate them precisely. Recognizing
'normal circumstances' (context) is thus crucial in detecting the
method-ical character of any activity, whether it presents itself
to us as an indexical or objective expression.

Doubtless the importance of context in recognizing and explaining individual cases was what Durkheim had in mind when
he noted the subjectivity that tends to be present the closer one
gets to individual facts. For *ad hocing* practices of the kind that
Wittgenstein mentions ('in normal circumstances' as an '*et cetera*
clause' contained in any instructions about the application of
rules) invariably are employed to relate instances to rules. Yet,
it is difficult to see why, if 'in normal circumstances' always
applies to the recognition of individual cases, it does not equally
apply to the recognition of regularities, e.g. suicide rates as
opposed to individual 'suicides'. For, unless suicide rates compile

themselves, they must be the product of some kind of human activity – by families, by coroners and, ultimately, by official statisticians as each tries to make some sense of either a dead body or of a mass of individual facts. Without paying 'proper' attention to '*et cetera*', 'let it pass', what 'must have been' the case, 'for all practical purposes', suicides would never get recorded and rates of suicide would never get compiled. For only in, and through, the practices of relevant persons (not, incidentally, including the presumed 'suicidee' who, after all, can no longer participate in the negotiation of 'the facts of the case') do suicides get recognized and rates get compiled.

Nowhere in this am I suggesting that recognizing a suicide is usually a *difficult* act. Anyone could do it – you as well as I. But we can do it because we are always already members: in detecting the method-ical character of an activity, we re-member our membership. As much as adherence to method seeks to negate our re-membering of self, or to see it as an unfortunate practice ('bias') which gets in the way of an 'objective representation', the human activity of the production of sense is always present.

Yet method always succeeds. It always allows us to distinguish between and move from indexical to objective expressions. Its success lies, however, never in its prescriptions, but always in our membership. As members, not only can we see the good sense of making a distinction between context-bound and context-free statements; we rely on making it. Like Castaneda, we would 'lose all rationality' if we could not distinguish 'the way we see things' from 'the way things really are' and have methods for establishing the exact character of the latter. In our confidence in such methods, in our conviction that we are being method-ical, we both guarantee the practical success of our activities and conceal the membership that always pre-figures and grounds the 'good sense' of what we see and do.

Method and concealment

The concealment of our-selves, inherent in adherence to method, means that, as we use method, it uses us. Heidegger makes the point this way:

The sciences know the way to knowledge by the term method.

Method, especially in today's modern scientific thought, is not a mere instrument serving the sciences; rather it has pressed the sciences into its own service. (1971, p. 74)

For Heidegger, method 'has pressed the sciences into its own service' because it makes scientists forgetful of their own presence within their texts. As with Castaneda's attempts to uncover the facts by employing various techniques, method allows scientists to be successful, while forgetting the fate-ful elections which their own activities express. Indeed, only in and through such forgetfulness *can* method be successful.

Method forgets that, like the phenomena it re-presents, an account comes to be recognized as 'orderly', 'proper' and 'objective' only through the 'appropriate' invocation of a body of unformulated common-sense practices, a body of practices which must remain unformulated because only the membership which they express *permits* their address and is thus *concealed* at each and every attempt to formulate them. So the 'objective' status of an account is no more protected by 'proper' adherence to method than is any activity – like suicide – governed by rules. For only through the membership which is always already present in understanding do accounts come to be recognized as in-accord-with-a-rule. So Castaneda, like Durkheim, fails to re-member the human and active character of his reading, fails to re-collect his social production of sense.

Writing, like reading, is equally an act of social production. For we do not write as automatons bound by method. Writing is never 'untouched by human hands'. Or rather that version only makes sense in terms of the modern attempt to make self-effacement the standard of seriousness of an activity. So to write under the auspices of method is to elect a certain mode of existence. It is to make what Marx has called a particular 'confession'. A confession which expresses self as a faceless bureaucrat who finds identity within the absence of self from text. An existence which expresses itself in a non-existence. So, to write (act) under the auspices of method (rule), is to find one's community among all those whose activities are the very denial of their humanity; who, like Eichmann, conceal them-selves behind method and rule.

Perhaps this self-forgetfulness lies in the identification of method with technique, in an assumption that, without technique, our accounts are not to be trusted, are, in some way, un-methodic. But what would a non-methodic account look like? Clearly, its lack of method would have to be described (constituted) as such by a publicly acceptable reading. And the way of knowledge which such a reading would exemplify could never itself be non-methodic, could never fail to provide for the orderly character of the world. No more than the writing could be produced without its internal display of its methodic character. For method is not something brought to writing (reading). It is always already there within a text's claim to intelligibility; within the possible society it proposes, within the self it re-collects.

Suggestions for further reading

Durkheim's two works, *The Rules of Sociological Method* (1964) and *Suicide* (1952), are both relatively easy to follow. They offer the classic formulation within sociology of the identification of method with technique. Later critical works which take up Durkheim's position include Paul Filmer, Michael Phillipson, David Silverman and David Walsh, *New Directions in Sociological Theory* (Filmer *et al.*, 1972) and Jack Douglas, *The Social Meanings of Suicide* (1970).

The distinction between 'indexical' and 'objective' expressions, as well as the notion of *ad hocing* practices, I take from Harold Garfinkel's *Studies in Ethnomethodology* (1967). My version of how both 'description' and 'method' constitute the character of what they address owes a great deal to his concept of 'reflexivity' developed in this book.

The way in which method, viewed as technique, allows us to see 'bias' as a problem which gets in the way of objective accounts, is addressed in the chapter called 'Bias' in McHugh *et al.*, *On the Beginning of Social Enquiry* (1974).

Jurgen Habermas's *Knowledge and Human Interests* (1972) likewise rejects technique and suggests what he calls a hermeneutic understanding which 'ties the interpreter to the role of a partner' in a dialogue (pp. 179-80).

4
Truth

> *Truth* (1) Agreement with that which is represented, cor-
> respondence to reality, verisimilitude . . .
> (2) Conformity to rule, exactness, correctness . . .
> (3) That which is true; that which conforms to fact or
> reality . . . as to seek the *truth*; the *truths* of science.
> (*Webster's Collegiate Dictionary*, fifth edition)

As we have seen, Castaneda's text consists, in large part, of a
presentation of his conversations with don Juan interpolated with
accounts of his activities and comments about his understandings.
Following this pattern, after an account of Castaneda's battle with
a fake don Juan, the main part of the book concludes with the
following observations:

> That experience was the last of don Juan's teachings. Ever
> since that time I have refrained from seeking his lessons. And,
> although don Juan has not changed his benefactor's attitude
> toward me, I do believe that I have succumbed to the first
> enemy of a man of knowledge. (p. 185)

Yet despite 'that experience' being 'the last of don Juan's teachings',
the book itself does not come to an end here. The account of
'experiences' and 'lessons' is followed by a second part – 'A
Structural Analysis'.

In his introduction, Castaneda explains the purpose of this
analysis:

In the second part of this book I present a structural analysis drawn exclusively from the data reported in the first part. Through my analysis I seek to support the following contentions: (1) don Juan presented his teachings as a system of logical thought; (2) the system made sense only if examined in the light of its structural units; and (3) the system was designed to guide an apprentice to a. level of conceptualization which explained the order of the phenomena he had experienced. (p. 25)

What is the sense of this 'second part'? After all, have we not already been given Castaneda's account, so why do we need his further 'contentions'?

I suggest that the requirement for a 'second part' and the character of the analysis contained within it both make entirely good sense as an exemplification of a simplified model of scientific enquiry. According to such a model, one must begin by gathering all available facts – notice how, for purposes of his 'structural analysis', Castaneda now refers to the first part of the book as 'data'. Once the data has been assembled, the enquirer will seek to generate an explanation, in terms of the scientific discipline in which he is trained, which is consistent with the data. Castaneda's 'second part', then, makes sense to me as an anthropological (i.e. expert) account which, by pulling the threads together from the earlier part of the book, seeks to convince both fellow-experts and the lay reader.

Why should we be convinced by Castaneda's 'structural analysis'? Because, in its orderly presentation of facts, in its systematic interlocking of concepts, it exemplifies its method-ical character. Given Castaneda's display of technique, we come to see his masterly control over the materials presented in the first part of the book. So the 'structural analysis' looks as though it stands on firmer grounds than do the earlier materials. After all, the first part is only reportage; now we are being presented with a scientific analysis, which, because it rests on a systematic application of technique rather than on mere impressions, can only be closer to the 'truth'. Indeed, Castaneda's 'structural analysis' speaks to us in precisely the terms of the dictionary version of 'truth' as:

Conformity to rule, exactness, correctness . . . .

Unlike the early accounts, the second part of the book does, indeed, present itself as in 'conformity to rule', and seems to have the qualities of 'exactness' and 'correctness'.

So, in his 'structural analysis', Castaneda claims to be taken seriously as an expert who can impose his will on even the most difficult 'data'. Given his expert knowledge, given his correct application of method, his text will show us the 'proper' sense of the materials. Part Two of the book thus reads to me as a legislation of how Part One must be read. Castaneda is seeking to persuade us that, if we recognize his 'proper' observance of method, then his account has to be the 'proper' interpretation. So, rather than address the character of his persuasive version of the world, Castaneda is persuaded by it and wants it to persuade us.

Castaneda is not blind to the possibility of bias in his own account:

> In spite of all the effort I have put forth to render these concepts as faithfully as possible, their meaning has been deflected by my own attempts to classify them. (p. 189)

Yet notice how his aim is always couched in an appeal to 'conformity to rule, exactness and correctness' – his 'effort' is unceasingly directed to the attempt 'to render these concepts as faithfully as possible'. So Castaneda's recognition of the possibility of 'bias' ('meaning' being 'deflected'), and his attempts to transcend it ('all the effort I have put forward') are both made intelligible by the commitment to method (viewed as technique) which his text displays. Such a commitment allows him to continue this passage with the following claim:

> The arrangement of the four main units of this structural scheme is, however, a logical sequence which appears to be free from the influence of extraneous classificatory devices of my own. (*ibid.*)

Consider Castaneda's characterization of his analysis as 'a logical sequence'. We are to be convinced, it would seem, because, after all, the text merely reflects the canons of 'logic' and the author

himself is quite absent from the writing – so the text 'appears to
be free from the influence of extraneous classificatory devices of
my own'.

But what, then, is the character of the first part of the book?
Is it illogical? In one sense, it might seem to be. For, if method
is technique, then Part One does read as more slap-dash, less
methodical, than Part Two. Yet, in another sense, the first part
cannot be il-logical, for it clearly makes sense to us and it also
seems to have made sense to Castaneda. What, then, are we to
make of his reference to the analysis in Part Two as a 'logical
sequence'? The intelligibility of this reference arises for me in a
way of speaking which assumes that the logic of a text always
remains to be explicated *outside* the text or that the meaning of
data always *awaits* explication. Hence, we rely on experts who
will show us the 'proper' understanding of the text or of the
'data'. So Castaneda's Part Two is always required in writing
that seeks to ground its sense in technique. Without its Part Two,
a text or 'data' is always non-methodical and requires 'proper'
analysis governed by the application of technique.

But what if analysis is always present in the text itself, always
present in the recognition of 'data'? What if the text, as an act
of production of sense, always displays the grounds of its intelligibility – its 'logic'? So we no longer need to go outside the text,
we no longer need a 'structural analysis', in order to be confronted with a method-ical presentation. For the text itself
sustains a system of intelligibility.

Only when method is equated with technique can any text be
recognized as un-methodic, or, in terms of the dictionary definition,
be 'un-true' – because it is not in 'conformity to rule', not 'exact'
and not 'correct'. Equally, our reading of the text will always be
our reading. Here, now, affirming a system of intelligibility for
which we are responsible, affirming the mode of existence in
which we produce our-selves. By presenting itself as a 'proper'
reading of his conversations, Castaneda's 'structural analysis' only
conceals, then, both the method-ical character of what he has
already written and our responsibility for what we make of any
part of his text. Yet, viewed as itself a text, as neither a develop-
ment nor an explication of the first part, his 'structural analysis'
does give us an occasion to re-member our version of 'truth'.

The reality of special consensus

Castaneda understands the truth of don Juan's teachings by reference to the notion of *'special consensus'*. In turn, 'special consensus' is produced in relation to periods of *'non-ordinary reality'*. Let me begin by examining the sense that Castaneda seems to give to each of these terms.

To transcend ordinary reality one needs an ally. The 'little smoke' was an ally, according to don Juan, because, as 'a power capable of transporting a man beyond the boundaries of himself', it allowed him to enter a state of 'non-ordinary reality'. Meetings with the ally thus constituted states of 'non-ordinary reality'. Castaneda uses this term:

> because it conformed with don Juan's assertion that such meetings took place in a continuum of reality, a reality that was only slightly different from the ordinary reality of everyday life. Consequently, non-ordinary reality had specific characteristics that could be assessed in presumably equal terms by everyone. (p. 208)

Notice how Castaneda stresses that 'non-ordinary' reality is not cut off from everyday life; meetings with the ally take place 'in a continuum of reality, a reality that [is] only slightly different from the ordinary reality of everyday life.' Neither is 'non-ordinary reality' experienced as a private state of mind – rather it has 'specific characteristics that could be assessed in presumably equal terms by everyone'.

The similarity between 'ordinary' and 'non-ordinary' reality arises in the *stability* of one's impressions in each state:

> The component elements of non-ordinary reality had stability in the sense that they were constant. In this respect they were similar to the component elements of ordinary reality, for they neither shifted nor disappeared, as would the component elements of ordinary dreams. It seemed as if every detail that made up a component element of non-ordinary reality had a concreteness of its own, a concreteness I perceived as extraordinarily stable. The stability was so pronounced that it allowed me to establish the criterion that, in non-ordinary reality, one always possessed the capacity to come to a halt

in order to examine any of the component elements for what appeared to be an indefinite length of time. (p. 209)

So, according to Castaneda, 'non-ordinary reality' is not comparable to a state of dreaming. It has 'a concreteness of its own, a concreteness that I perceived as extraordinarily stable'. This concreteness is reflected in an ability to focus and re-focus at will on particular elements for any length of time ('the capacity to come to a halt'). As when viewing everyday events through the lens of a camera, in 'non-ordinary reality' one can use a different mental lens to re-focus on a different aspect of the scene, while remaining confident that the original aspect would remain stable while one was not looking at it and that, if one so desired, one could view it again at a later time. So 'non-ordinary reality' has the kind of stability that convinces us, in everyday life, that a picture does not disappear from a wall just because we no longer have it within our gaze.

'Non-ordinary reality' is, however, according to Castaneda, not entirely the same as the reality of the everyday world. While its stability distinguishes it from other states of 'peculiar perception' (like dreams), its *singularity* and *lack of ordinary consensus* differentiate it from 'ordinary reality'. Its 'singularity' meant that:

> every detail of the component elements was a single, individual item; it seemed as if each detail was isolated from others, or as if details appeared one at a time. The singularity of the component elements seemed further to create a unique necessity, which may have been common to everybody: the imperative need, the urge, to amalgamate all isolated details into a total scene, a total composite. (*ibid.*)

So, in 'non-ordinary reality', one is conscious of the lack of relation (or 'singularity') of all the details one sees. At the same time, the fact that each element seems to stand out on its own seems to create 'a need' 'to amalgamate all isolated details into a total scene, a total composite'. Yet, perhaps, in everyday life things only seem already related because we take for granted our ways of relating them and the typical 'patterns' that these ways give rise to. For instance, on walking into a room, we typically don't notice individual objects except in the context of

our seen but unnoticed recognition that it is a particular kind of
room – a living-room, a kitchen, etc. So the 'singularity' of non-
ordinary reality, for Castaneda, may have been a feature of his
lack of familiarity with the 'patterns' to expect. As a consequence,
he is more conscious of his own acts of 'amalgamation' and
'composition'.

This inability to take for granted the 'patterns' available in 'non-
ordinary reality' is reflected in Castaneda's attribution to it of a
lack of ordinary consensus. He writes about this in the following
passage:

> The third unique characteristic of the component elements, and
> the most dramatic of all, was their lack of ordinary consensus.
> One perceived the component elements while being in a state
> of complete solitude, which was more like the aloneness of a
> man witnessing by himself an unfamiliar scene in ordinary
> reality than like the solitude of dreaming. As the stability of
> the component elements of non-ordinary reality enabled one
> to stop and examine any of them for what appeared to be an
> indefinite length of time, it seemed almost as if they were
> elements of everyday life; however, the difference between the
> component elements of the two states of reality was their
> capacity for ordinary consensus. *By ordinary consensus I mean
> the tacit or implicit agreement on the component elements of every-
> day life which fellow men give to one another in various ways.
> For the component element of non-ordinary reality, ordinary con-
> sensus was unattainable.* In this respect non-ordinary reality was
> closer to a state of dreaming than to ordinary reality. And yet,
> because of their unique characteristics of stability and singu-
> larity, the component elements of non-ordinary reality had a
> compelling quality of realness which seemed to foster the
> necessity of validating their existence in terms of consensus.
> (pp. 209-10)

When Castaneda writes that 'non-ordinary reality' lacks ordinary
consensus, I think he is referring less to physical separation
from others who might support one's impressions than to an
absence of taken-for-granted ways of understanding, an absence
that would be felt even in the presence of other men. Perhaps
this can be expressed in terms of the phrase 'to trust one's

senses'. In 'non-ordinary reality', because there is no 'tacit or implicit agreement on the component elements of everyday life', one cannot trust one's senses. So the absence that Castaneda experiences is not the absence of persons (non-ordinary reality is not 'like the solitude of dreaming'), but the absence of communally warranted ways of making sense. Without the secure 'knowing' sustained by a way ·of knowledge, non-ordinary reality is experienced as a set of individual sensations. Lacking 'knowledge', one cannot trust one's senses. So a man has the experience of 'witnessing by himself' (apart from a communal way of knowledge) 'an unfamiliar scene' (experiencing sense impressions but lacking an ability to 'know' that the events they depicted were 'really happening').

Yet, in writing about non-ordinary reality, Castaneda makes it clear that the world one experiences as non-ordinary is not a private world. For, in so far as it has a *reality*, people experience it as a stable, solid and factual world – 'the way things are' – which, like the picture on the wall, will not go away when we cease to look at it. So, to the extent that this non-ordinary state is 'real', it must be a public world, sustained by communal practices for recognizing, describing and explaining it. 'Special consensus' is the term which Castaneda gives to the practice which sustained non-ordinary reality:

> In don Juan's teachings, special consensus meant tacit or implicit agreement on the component elements of non-ordinary reality, which he, in his capacity as teacher, gave me as the apprentice of his knowledge. (p. 215)

This 'agreement on the component elements of non-ordinary reality' meant that Castaneda learnt the background understandings against which any non-ordinary experience would be visible and comprehensible. Given these understandings, he would no longer *sense* that something was happening to him, he would *know* that something was really the case.

The character of this 'special consensus' was negotiated between don Juan and Castaneda. According to Castaneda, in these negotiations don Juan would perform the tasks of 'preparing the background' for 'special consensus' and 'guiding' it. 'Preparing the background' was achieved by getting Castaneda to participate

in certain special states of *ordinary* reality which don Juan seemed
to have produced himself. Despite the fact that don Juan never
claimed to have done so, it seemed to Castaneda:

> that he produced them [special states of ordinary reality]
> through a skilful manipulation of hints and suggestions to
> guide my behaviour. I have called that process the 'manipula-
> tion of cues'. (p. 218)

By means of suggestion, don Juan would isolate a component
element of ordinary reality (a colour, Castaneda's initial impression
of him) and, through a skilful line of questioning, confuse Castaneda's routine way of recognizing such an element. A new and
incongruous element would now be perceived by Castaneda – an
element which could not be subjected to ordinary consensus.
Only don Juan, as the teacher, could warrant knowledge as to
the new 'facts of the matter':

> don Juan, as the coparticipant of that special state of ordinary
> reality, was the only person who knew what the component
> elements were, and thus he was the only person who could
> give me agreement on their existence. (p. 219)

Castaneda needed that 'agreement' if he were to escape his feeling
of uncertainty and disarray. Yet, according to him, don Juan
both created that uncertainty and determined how it should be
resolved.

Don Juan's 'manipulation of cues' was also observed by Castaneda in the way in which the former expounded on Castaneda's
recapitulation of his experiences at the aftermath of each state
of non-ordinary reality. Don Juan would regularly emphasize
certain aspects of Castaneda's accounts, by centring on them the
bulk of his speculation in terms of the goals he had expected to
be achieved in the state of non-ordinary reality. This process of
selective emphasis also had another side – selective de-emphasis:

> The second selective process that don Juan employed was to
> deny all importance to some areas of my account. I have called
> it 'lack of emphasis' because it was the opposite and the counter-
> balance of emphasis. It seemed that by denying importance to
> the parts of my account pertaining to component elements

which don Juan judged to be completely superfluous to the
goal of his teachings, he literally obliterated my perception of
the same elements in the successive states of non-ordinary
reality. (p. 221)

The practice of 'obliterating perception' which occurred in
'preparing the background' for 'special consensus' served to
dis-attach Castaneda from his commitment to the 'ordinary consensus' appropriate to 'ordinary reality'. Castaneda could no
longer trust his senses to recognize and understand a familiar
world. Given Castaneda's new-found doubts and uncertainties,
don Juan could now assert an alternative, but no less stable, way
of producing sense. He now 'guided' Castaneda to an understanding of the component elements of non-ordinary reality.
Castaneda now perceived progressively unfamiliar forms (in terms
of ordinary reality) and patterns of relationship between forms.
He perceived far more complex detail in the forms he observed.
He writes of his:

impressions of vague forms during the early states to my perception of massive elaborate arrays of minute particulars in the
late states. (p. 225)

But, as well as seeing 'massive elaborate arrays of minute particulars', he became able to perceive a far wider range of forms.
The whole area over which he could exert his capacity to focus
attention seemed to expand.

At this point, Castaneda's acceptance of another way of seeing,
influenced by what he calls the 'manipulation of cues', seems to
suggest that he has been the target of an elaborate confidence
trick. Perhaps he was. Perhaps the movement from one way of
seeing to the other was a skilful manipulative process. But we
should not leap to the conclusion that the 'non-ordinary reality'
of 'special consensus' was any less real than the 'ordinary reality'
of 'ordinary consensus'. Castaneda specifically denies this and
continually asserts that living in non-ordinary reality was not at
all like the 'fake' life of a dream. 'Non-ordinary reality', to those
who experienced it, was undeniably really 'real'. It was not a
figment of don Juan's imagination; it did not relate only to his

private, idiosyncratic sensations. To see it and live in it was to experience a stable, organized world, which, because of its factual character, was resistant to individual intentions. Such a world offered both resources and troubles to those who dwelled within it. Moreover, to dwell within it, as to dwell within 'ordinary reality', was not simply to *sense* that something might be the case but to *know* that something had to be the case.

To speak the language which exemplified a Yaqui way of knowledge was, then, to propose the possible society of non-ordinary reality. In and through 'special consensus', that possible society was proposed and created as *the* society – as 'the way things were'. To be a member of that society was to have knowledge; to have knowledge was to be a member.

To have particular details of knowledge and to understand particular truths already pre-supposes the membership (the communality) which makes particular knowledge and truths accessible to human understanding. So members recognize particular truths in the context of their way of knowledge which, as the expression of their mode of existence, is the bedrock of all truth for them. A bedrock which clears the space in which particular truths can be experienced. So truth can only be secure in the election of a certain mode of existence. And particular truths are only made available in the context of communally warranted practices for asserting and conceding the valid character of truth-claims on the occasion at which such claims are made. To know (that something is true or false) always implies that one knows already (the mode of existence which grounds truth); it always implies a prior area of openness in which truth is accessible.

Community always searches for one's speech; one's speech always searches for community. Castaneda's movement to an existence in non-ordinary reality reflects not simply the forcefulness of don Juan's 'manipulation of cues' but Castaneda's own recognition that there is no half-way house between the two realities. Between the states of ordinary reality verified by ordinary consensus and non-ordinary reality verified by special consensus, any uncommitted position is illusory. In noting that the component elements of non-ordinary reality were not to be recognized by trusting one's (ordinary) senses, Castaneda makes much the same point. He writes:

those component elements were not subject to ordinary consensus, and if one was incapable of obtaining agreement on their existence, their perceived realness would have been only an illusion. As a man would have to be by himself in nonordinary reality, by reason of his solitariness whatever he perceived would have to be idiosyncratic. The solitariness and the idiosyncrasies were a consequence of the assumed fact that no fellow-man could give one ordinary consensus on one's perceptions. (p. 214)

Without communally sanctioned means of 'obtaining agreement on [the] existence' of the component elements of non-ordinary reality, they would lose all their factual character, all their reality ('their perceived realness would have been only an illusion'). For, as Castaneda reminds us, facts and truths only exist in and for communities. But, as he points out, the absence of a claim to community within one's speech produces only a 'solitary', 'idiosyncratic' world. Which is to say it produces an unthinkable world, a world which is only mine and not yours, a world which cannot be thought because, in thinking, we express our communality.

Whatever passes for truth reflects communal practices which constitute the character of particular truths for that community. Through our ability to recognize and to invoke such practices, we express our membership and provide ourselves with knowledge which is always more than an individual's sensations. So knowledge is a collective product and 'knowing' a collective act. Peter McHugh puts it this way:

The difference between *sensing* and *knowing* is the one between *private* psychological perception (or misperception) and collective *public* truth. ('On the failure of positivism', in Douglas, 1971, p. 331, emphasis mine)

Particular truths are always located by public recognition of the 'validity', 'good sense', or whatever, of a proposition or assumption. The scientist senses a relationship between two variables but science, as an institution, by its concession or denial of the truth of the relationship, concedes or denies its status as knowledge which can be admitted to its collective body of truths. So the scientist doesn't *sense* that water is composed of two parts

F

hydrogen to one part oxygen, he already *knows* that such is the case. For such knowledge is a feature of his commitment to his community; it is his community. Which is not to say that the community will dissolve should that knowledge be later judged refuted. Rather, in collectively conceding and denying truth-claims, in collectively affirming certain knowledge and certain methods for recognizing knowledge, scientists affirm their community.

While each community knows its methods for recognizing truths, the relation between these methods and the concession (or denial) of a particular truth is always negotiated at every instance. The truth of a statement is never independent of its utterance, an utterance which is recognized as, for all practical purposes, letting other considerations pass, *et cetera*, in-accord-with-a-communally-sanctioned-method. So particular truths are always products of a community's truth-conferring activities. In this sense, McHugh writes later, that 'truth' is a 'behavioural accomplishment'. An accomplishment which expresses and sustains community by its necessary underlying appeals to what Durkheim referred to as all 'honest observers' – where to be 'honest' and to be an 'observer' presupposes one's membership of a community from which such truth-claims may be produced and to which they are addressed.

If this suggests a certain circularity, that is all to the good. Speech provides for the system of intelligibility within which it becomes 'true'. So the truth-claims of speech propose a community in which they may be judged. For instance, when I say:

* 'I'm feeling rather tired today',

I appeal to my own sense of my feelings. Others may tell me I don't look tired and a doctor may indicate that there is nothing medically wrong with me, but this is unlikely to shake my faith in my sense of the truth of my statement for me. After all, the statement proposes that it only refers to my private state and I am, presumably, the best judge of that (although in recognizing 'private states', we affirm the publicly sharable language-game of 'talking-about-sensations').

Alternatively, when I propose:

* 'Two and two make five',

I will be taken to be referring to an arithmetical proposition which will hold (or not) outside my individual perceptions. Hence, because my speech reads (for us) as referring not to 'the way I see things' but to 'the way things are', others may step in and appeal to publicly available 'knowledge' as means of conceding or refuting my proposition. And it would be rather strange for me to reply in this case (but not at all strange in the former case):

* 'Well, but that's not how I see things.'

To see the good sense of my first proposition and to deny the good sense (or truth) of the second one is to affirm a shared commitment of speaker and hearer to that world (and hence to that way of knowledge) which distinguishes private states from publicly knowable truths. On the other hand, to deny that I can judge my private state, or to affirm that personal opinion can settle the sum of two plus two, only 'refutes' the truths which my speech proposes by appealing to (re-collecting) another world. Hence, while (routinely) community is affirmed in the refutation of statements, in denying the communal knowledge in and through which truth-claims are conceded, *this kind of refutation* merely re-presents another system of intelligibility.

What both these cases share in common is that the sanctioning of truth-claims always expresses a possible society – a society which the truth-claim itself appeals to or, sometimes, a society which will be recognizably insane to the other speaker (as a society in which personal opinion could settle the sum of two plus two would be insane for us). When proposing or judging truth-claims, we are, then, proposing possible societies. As Alan Blum argues:

> In our conceptual explorations we are not stripping the events of the world down to their bare essences, rather we are using these events of the world to show our version of language and life. ('Theorizing', in Douglas, 1971, p. 317)

In recognizing the good sense of statements, we re-collect the society which grounds the good sense of our statements. Rather than tell us more about the other's speech (its 'bare essence'), our speech 'shows' the possible society in which we elect to live (shows 'our version of language and life').

As Blum points out later in the same paper, communities express themselves in their members' preparedness to stop doubting at a particular point. So, in refusing to doubt that I can be the judge of my private state, I affirm my commitment to the way of knowledge which constitutes, what Castaneda calls, 'ordinary reality'. Similarly, in eventually refusing to doubt the factual character of 'non-ordinary reality', he affirms his commitment to the factual world which it proposes. This is a far deeper commitment than that expressed in a preparedness simply to accept one or two of don Juan's propositions. In accepting the reality of 'non-ordinary reality', Castaneda must accept 'special consensus' as the framework which allows propositions to be recognized, let alone validated. It is no longer a case of choosing to accept some of don Juan's more appealing propositions. This is still the posture of the outsider who only 'sees' and 'understands' from within a secure framework which he will never address. To enter fully into 'non-ordinary reality', 'special consensus' must be Castaneda's *only* path to truth. And to accept the grounding of all truths in 'special consensus', Castaneda must accept the *totality* of the special consensus given to all the elements of the states of 'non-ordinary reality' and to all the special states of 'ordinary reality'. He puts it this way:

> the acceptance of special consensus meant for me, as the apprentice, the adoption of a certain point of view validated by the totality of don Juan's teachings; that is, it meant my entrance into a conceptual level, a level comprising an order of conceptualization that would render the teachings understandable in their own terms. I have called it the 'conceptual order' because it was the order that gave meaning to the unordinary phenomena that formed don Juan's knowledge; it was the matrix of meaning in which all individual concepts brought out in his teachings were embedded. (pp. 227-8)

The 'conceptual order' which Castaneda enters is more than a collection of opinions or facts; rather it is the basis for recognizing 'opinions' or 'facts'. So to live in 'non-ordinary reality' is to experience the truths of 'non-ordinary reality' grounded in the truth of 'special consensus'. There is no 'independent' way to test these truths. Or rather, any apparently 'independent' way merely proposes another 'conceptual order', merely re-members another possible society.

To live in the possible society proposed by special consensus is ultimately to deny the 'non-ordinary' character of its reality. For each successive experience confirms the 'conceptual order' in terms of which it is recognized. What was originally viewed as the 'way things might be' now inescapably and inexorably becomes 'the way things are', as the 'conceptual order' and the experience validate each other. What originally presented itself as strange and 'non-ordinary' now seems routine and 'ordinary':

> I use the term 'non-ordinary reality', as already noted, in the sense of extraordinary, uncommon reality. For a beginner apprentice such a reality was by all means unordinary, but the apprenticeship of don Juan's knowledge demanded my compulsory participation and my commitment to pragmatic and experimental practice of whatever I had learned. That meant that I, as the apprentice, had to experience a number of states of non-ordinary reality, and that *first-hand knowledge would, sooner or later, make the classifications 'ordinary' and 'non-ordinary' meaningless for me.* The bona fide adoption of the first unit of the conceptual order would have entailed, then, the idea that there was another separate, but no longer unordinary, realm of reality, the 'reality of special consensus'. (pp. 230-1, emphasis mine)

Given Castaneda's 'first-hand knowledge' of 'non-ordinary reality', it simply becomes a 'reality' for him, separate from everyday reality 'but no longer unordinary'. This reality, the 'reality of special consensus', is unmistakably 'real' – in and through the practices of 'special consensus'. These practices make truth accessible to the enquirer by opening up the space in which particular truths can be recognized.

So the 'reality of special consensus' exists through (as) the practices of 'special consensus'. These practices are its own language for talking about itself. *They are itself.* Consequently, in terms of these practices, the 'reality of special consensus' is always experienced as really 'real'. As Castaneda tells us, its reality was not at all dream-like:

The acceptance of special consensus on all the states of non-ordinary reality, and on all the special states of ordinary reality, was designed to consolidate the awareness that it was equal to the reality of ordinary, everyday-life consensus. This equality was based on the impression that the reality of special consensus was not a realm that could be equated with dreams. On the contrary, it had stable component elements that were subject to special agreement. It was actually a realm where one could perceive the surroundings in a deliberate manner. Its component elements were not idiosyncratic or whimsical, but concise items or events whose existence was attested to by the whole body of teachings. (p. 231)

The 'stability' of its component elements, the possibility of perceiving the surroundings 'in a deliberate manner', make Castaneda experience the 'reality of special consensus' as entirely 'equal to the reality of ordinary, everyday-life consensus'. In experiencing its reality, Castaneda elects to live his life differently. He re-members his mode of existence by claiming community with a possible society that is not his own concrete society.

For us, then, Castaneda, in experiencing the factual, real character of 'non-ordinary reality', becomes crazy or deluded. For his talk, his understandings, seem to propose a crazy society. Yet, within his dialogues with don Juan, Castaneda is defined as less and less crazy the more he comes to appreciate the 'reality of special consensus'. For don Juan, Castaneda's talk then begins to propose a possible society which *is* their way of relating to each other. So Castaneda's talk comes to make sense for don Juan because, in proposing that knowledge is only to be located in terms of 'special consensus', it both expresses and constitutes the character of their relationship. The way of knowledge makes sense because it is their way of relating to each other; the 'reality of special consensus' is how they live their lives together. In the same way as, Wittgenstein tells us, an arrow points because it could do nothing else (for us), the form of life of 'special consensus' is the bedrock of the way of knowledge with which Castaneda is confronted. So, in terms of that way, Mescalito is both real and a teacher, because he could be nothing else. To see Mescalito otherwise, or not to see him at all, is only to be wrong or even crazy because such seeing proposes another possible society.

Truth and community

The 'reality of special consensus', in the reading which I have just offered to you, implies the public, communal character of truth. Truth is never a feature of the sensations of a discrete individual; it is always to be recognized in the knowledge of members of communities. Yet, if we look at the dictionary definition, truth seems to be just a question of an individual gathering data by his own senses and testing its correspondence with reality:

> *Truth* – Agreement with that which is represented, correspond-ence to reality, verisimilitude . . .

In terms of this definition, we hear no suggestion of the member-ship expressed in any act of re-presentation or of agreement. Truth, it would seem, can be an entirely private affair, established by an individual in, to use salesman's language, 'the privacy of his own home'.

Let us examine the 'good sense' of this proposition. It provides for the recognition of the following: (1) an observer with senses; (2) a world of objects; (3) the observer gathers sense-data about these objects and makes an assertion about them; and (4) the assertion is true if there is an object which corresponds to it. This is a crude re-presentation of what is sometimes called the 'correspondence' theory of truth – a theory which is expressed in summary form in proposition (4). Correspondence theory comes in several versions. Following McHugh, I want to con-sider briefly only two of these versions – truth is a 'copy' and truth is a 'test'.

If truth is a copy, then these statements are true which copy or picture some object(s) in the real world; statements which, in terms of the dictionary, are in 'correspondence to reality'. Now the 'copy' theory seems to make a great deal of sense when state-ments refer to material objects. For instance, if I say 'this is a table' and point towards an object, the truth of my statement, one feels, can be tested by looking in the direction in which I am pointing and observing whether there is really a table there. But what objects in the world correspond to 'Hello' or 'Perhaps'? Or, to put it another way, what do these words 'picture'? Again, what happens if I should keep on, relentlessly, saying: 'It's a table, it's a table, it's a table'? Whether or not there is an object at hand which seems to correspond to my words, my utterance may no longer be taken to picture an object. For its assessment as true (i.e. as a correct picture) or otherwise seems inappropriate when 'anyone can see' that it is not 'really' a 'statement' but much more like a 'joke', 'childish chatter', or an expression of 'mania'. In any event, the sense of my utterance will reside not in my intentions (e.g. as a statement) but in the practices through which others come to recognize its sense (e.g. as a joke).

So the recognition of a truth-claim lies not in whether a statement 'actually' copies reality but in whether it is taken to represent reality, in the context in which it is uttered, by the community to whom it is addressed. That community warrants not only the truthfulness of particular statements but the recognition of a world which those statements are supposed to copy. So, to continue with my example, the table is only 'there', available to be re-presented, in and through the ways of speaking, the form of life, of particular communities.

The dependence of the 'copy' theory of truth upon the debate about the character of reality has made it rather unfashionable recently. As I suggested in the last chapter, contemporary scientists, like Durkheim, usually prefer to side-step positions which involve them in endless metaphysical debates. As a consequence, a version of truth has arisen which makes, apparently, no claims about 'reality' or the extent to which statements copy it or picture it. According to this version, true ideas are simply those we cannot refute after all reasonable efforts. Truth is now a 'test' rather than a 'copy'. True statements are to be recognized in their correct application of method, rather than in their correspondence to 'reality'. To be true is now to be method-ical where truth arises in:

Conformity to rule, exactness, correctness.

The solution to the metaphysical problem that this version of truth offers, however, only succeeds by a forgetfulness of the metaphysical implications of its own position. For what are the grounds of the assertion (conviction?) that 'truth is a test'? Clearly, they cannot be the same as it offers itself for the evaluation of statements. If the assertion that true ideas are those we cannot refute is valid, then it refutes the refutability principle. For it cannot be refuted itself. Alternatively, we must treat the refutability principle as a nonsense, without any basis for truthfulness.

Yet, clearly, the position that truth is a test does make sense to us and, equally, is the position that underlies the truth-claims of many scientific papers. So, rather than take the stand that it is il-logical, rather than try to destroy it, we must preserve it, we must understand its 'good sense'. For any attempt to destroy it through 'logic' would merely reinforce the basis of its sense – that to be truth-ful is to be method-ical. And this basis is more than an assumption which the scientific community happens to use. Rather in method (viewed as technique), the community finds itself – 'is' itself. Method is its mode of existence. So, in locating truth in adherence to method, in warranting that, for all practical purposes, 'all reasonable efforts' have been made to refute an assertion, such communities (scientists, bureaucrats, us (?)) produce themselves.

So, as we examine the identification of truth with correct method, we move away from private psychological perception to the collective public truth which re-presents the world we live in. This 'collective public truth' means that particular truths are always recognized within (as) the system of intelligibility of a community. Truths are always for and within a community, a community which may warrant certain methods as the basis for the production and recognition of truth-ful assertions ('testing', adhering to 'what everyone knows to be the case', respecting the 'reality of special consensus').

Yet, to make a successful truth-claim, these methods need not actually govern an assertion. How an assertion is produced is irrelevant to its success as a truth-claim. Or rather, what matters for its success is that some community recognize it as in-accord-with-warranted-methods. In turn, (community) members produce assertions for each other which seek to display that their assertions are indeed in-accord-with-warranted-methods.

To illustrate this method-ical character of particular truths, I

am going to consider a study by Zimmerman (1966) of the activities
of caseworkers at a district office of an American state bureau of
public assistance. Before welfare aid can be given, workers have
to establish a 'need', make a decision about the 'eligibility' of the
applicant in terms of that need and be able to justify that decision
in terms of the official requirements of the welfare programme in
question. The applicant first appears before a receptionist who
finds the 'relevant' form and 'clears' the case for the caseworker
by seeing to it that a complete and competent application is
executed, by assembling forms into a dossier, and by assigning
a caseworker to attend to the case. Only then does the documentation and investigation of the applicant's case begin. In these
activities, the caseworker adopts procedures and gives accounts
which both provide for and rely upon a sense of social structure.
The issue for Zimmerman, then, is not the reliability of these
procedures, nor the factual character of such accounts, but rather
the way in which both provide for their 'reliability' and 'factual
character'.

The intake caseworker's task is to assemble and assess information relevant to the applicant's eligibility for assistance. One of
the features of this activity, Zimmerman notes, is a treatment of
the applicant's 'story' as a set of claims which do not stand as
'facts' until they are verified. On the other hand, the 'story' is
allowed to stand as a 'fact', where it is seen to have a bearing on
a person's ineligibility for assistance – it is presumed that applicants would not invent particulars which might cast doubt on
their eligibility. In order to verify applicants' claims, caseworkers
marshal evidence drawn from official records (birth certificates,
medical records, details of encounters with other agencies, etc.).
However, while verbal statements are checked by reference to
pieces of paper, clearly not any piece of paper will do. For
instance, Zimmerman refers to an anecdote told by an intake
caseworker about an applicant who said she could not find the
citizenship papers giving her age but that she had at one time
copied her date of birth and given it to the caseworker. The other
caseworkers, he notes, found this story highly amusing – while
paper verification is important, it seems, only official papers will
serve that purpose.

On the basis of such search activity, caseworkers build up a dossier (a 'case record') which narrates the 'case' in terms of relevant transactions with the applicant, makes judgments about their significance in terms of questions of eligibility, and thereby prepares the ground for official action. The case record thus involves a transformation of history in terms of the relevancies of bureaucratic procedures. It does this, first, by allowing the applicant's history to be seen in terms of eligibility factors – thereby making her affairs, for bureaucratic purposes, into a case, and herself into a client; second, by displaying the caseworker's course of investigation as an activity in accord with legitimate organizational procedures, i.e. as demonstrably in-accord-with-a-rule. The caseworker's activities serve, then, both to assemble a world and to display its rule-governed character:

> The process of assembling a case record proceeds over a series of steps, each one informing the preceding. For reception and casework personnel alike, these steps are features of ordinary work practice which they make happen as observable events over a variety of occasions of concerted work, mutual instruction, discussion, and dispute. The way they are made to happen as observable events is a feature of the work of reconstruction.

As Zimmerman points out, the meaning of the past is found in the present (for caseworkers and bureaucrats alike, each step informs the preceding one).

The investigative stance of the intake caseworker is a thoroughgoing scepticism. Such scepticism serves to display the rationality of her actions. Even if her assumption that clients' claims (in themselves) have no basis turns out to be misguided in a particular instance, this is of no consequence, since claims have to be 'proved' in any event:

> From the point of view of experienced personnel, the 'stance' consists of a thorough-going scepticism directed to the applicant's claim to be eligible for assistance. As a mode of conducting an investigation, it is encountered in the setting by the observer (and by new personnel) as characterizations of 'good work', and as advice extended by supervisors and 'old hands' to novices, i.e. to those whose competence as caseworkers is problematic. In relation to the intake worker's task of making

the investigation of eligibility an accountably rational enterprise, 'being sceptical' is a way of displaying a hard-headed
commitment to establishing the 'facts of the matter' (as against
the applicant's mere *claims*) as well as being a method for
locating the courses of documentation which will determine the
relevant facts.

While new caseworkers often want to believe the claims of certain
clients, their supervisor's insistence that the intake function
should be treated as an investigative process, together with
personal experience with situations which run counter to applicants' claims and the workers' initial assessment, means that
workers soon learn a more 'acceptable' stance. In their actions,
the investigative stance is expressed in the practices of, first,
evoking the features of a setting which are investigatable matters
(can be settled by a document), and, second, in using typifications
of actors and settings in order to pick holes in applicants' accounts
(for instance, by asking: 'Is that what you would reasonably expect
a person needing help to do?'). Moreover, in their accounts and
records, the investigative stance is an even more obvious feature.
Zimmerman reports that in keeping records and talking to
colleagues, caseworkers displayed the central feature of their task
as the documentation of claims, thereby providing for a potential
discrepancy between the applicant's 'subjective' and 'interested'
claims and 'factual' and 'objective' records.
    Speed as well as 'verification' is also central to the intake case-
worker's activities. Not only do workers want to keep their case-
loads at a manageable level, they also seek to avoid having any
case 'unresolved' after thirty days – at which point it becomes
'delinquent' and official remedies become applicable. As a consequence, they pressure applicants to produce documentation to
support their claims and, having obtained such papers, treat
official records as self-evidently 'plain facts'. The problematic
status assigned to applicants' claims does not imply routinely
expressed open disbelief; indeed, where the applicant is 'co-
operative' (i.e. respects the bureaucratic relevances of the encounter and produces documentary evidence to support her
claims), the transaction can proceed quite 'smoothly'. Rather
caseworkers do not even conceive of the possibility that official

records might regularly be wrong or systematically falsified and attend to an applicant's talk on this basis. In their encounters with applicants, then, workers rely on this aspect of their sense of social structure to produce (for them) non-problematic situations. As Zimmerman argues, members' accounting is a feature of the setting it describes. By providing for the 'sense' of what it accounts, it constitutes the recognizable character of the phenomenon.

The status of official documents as 'plain facts' is accomplished, first, by seeing certain activities in society as *constituted* by record-keeping; in the cases of getting married or signing a property contract, for instance, the activity is necessarily linked to the record-keeping enterprise. Second, caseworkers ascribe typical motives to both the parties referred to in documents (who may be taken to intend what they do) and to bureaucratic record-keepers (who are taken to be detached, objective, and so on). For instance, an applicant's claim for unemployment benefit was jeopardized because his claim to have diligently sought work could not be 'verified'. Yet the lack of any record, Zimmerman suggests, might have reflected a lack of interest by organizations offering employment in recording casual and unsuccessful requests for work. However, from within the 'plain facts' perspective, there is no basis for doubting the routine reliability of official documents and the ordered properties of the world that they depict and rely upon:

> The taken-for-granted use of documents, as analysed by accounts given in the setting, is dependent on an ordered world – the ordered world of organizations, and the ordered world of the society-at-large. When simply taken-for-granted, the features of these ordered domains are matters of mere recognition for which no accounts are called for or given. Indeed, such routine recognition, and the action and inference proceeding from it, is the mark of the competent worker.

Both these activities and their outcomes are to the participants (and to the observer trying to make some sense out of agency records) non-problematic outcomes of a largely non-problematic world. Indeed, the end result, as Zimmerman remarks, provides a built-in assumption of its 'taken-for-granted' character.

Yet this is not to imply an ironic comparison between the 'documented' case and the actual state of affairs. The caseworkers' accounts are, in themselves, neither 'good' nor 'bad', neither 'unbiased' nor 'biased', neither 'accurate' nor 'inaccurate'. Rather they 'strike us' in this way to the extent that we identify truth with correct method – to the extent we elect to express our-selves within a bureaucratic mode of existence. In providing for their work to be seen as 'good', 'unbiased' and 'accurate', by displaying that their activities are, indeed, in-accord-with-warranted-methods, the caseworkers affirm their commitments to a mode of existence; they produce themselves as bureaucrats. So their actions come to be seen as 'correct' and their accounts are recognizably 'truthful' because, *as bureaucrats too*, we warrant particular truths as an expression of:

Conformity to rule, exactness, correctness.

Truth and particular truths

In the discussion of 'description', I suggested that Castaneda's problems of incomprehension could be re-presented through a distinction upon which our accounts seem to trade. This is the distinction between 'the way we see things' (subjectivity) and 'the way things really are' (objectivity). In terms of 'truth', this allows the distinction between the subjective mode of truth as a personally valid experience and the objective claims of truth as statements which 'copy' the world or are the outcome of proper 'test'. The former mode, *and* the latter, both assume that the basis for observations is the sense-impressions of an observer, while the latter stresses the need for those impressions to comply with a world of independent objects.

Yet these views of truth (and the subjective/objective distinction upon which they are based) are forgetful that particular truths are always grounded in the practices through which we produce and affirm our community. In recognizing the truthfulness of a *particular* statement, in *this* context, individuals express their community and define their mode of existence. So the truth of any utterance, like:

* 'I feel cold, or * 'Two plus two equals four', or * 'That is a table',

arises for and within the communities into which we collect our-
selves through the mode of intelligibility which our language
proposes. By speaking 'sensibly' and hearing the 'good sense' of
utterances, we express the membership that always grounds any
truth-claim.

Does this mean that *any* idea is permitted, if individuals happen
to believe that it is in 'correspondence' with the world or happen
to judge it to be in-accord-with-warranted-methods? Yes. But
not any truth-claim will succeed, nor will any means of warranting
truth do. For our means of warranting truth are expressions of the
way we live our lives together – they *are* our lives together. So
the basis for making and conceding truth-claims is the public
language of a community. And this could not be further from the
'relativistic' position that, since all assertions are relative to a
particular way of knowledge, there is no difference between
'truth' and 'falsity'. As Wittgenstein reminds us, it is through
notions of truth and falsity that we live our lives together. So,
of course, we *can* assert that there is no difference between the
two (language, after all, is not a prison), but, in doing so, we would
be proposing a non-existent society. For, to see no difference
between truth and falsity is for us, on most occasions, to be
recognizably crazy.

Yet, in judging the truth and falsity of particular utterances,
communities are invariably forgetful of the openness within
which particular truths manifest themselves. So the act of judgment, while producing a decision (true or false) about the character
of a particular assertion, always produces a concealment. Perhaps
this concealment arises because of our conviction that the role of
speech is to persuade an audience – to produce a community
that will be prepared to concede that the speech is truthful
because it is properly method-ical. But why seek to persuade?
Indeed, perhaps the very attempt to *generate* community by our
speech makes us forgetful of the community (the method, the
truth) that is always already there within our speech. For our
acts of seeing (vision) always express a commitment to a mode
of existence which provides the openness in which the seeing
gets done (a pro-vision). Before there is any-thing to which
our thinking can correspond, before there are particular truths,
our speech already appropriates truth by the community it

remembers. To listen to our own language is to hear that community within our speech.

Suggestions for further reading

My treatment of the versions of truth as a 'copy' and as a 'test' owes a great deal to Peter McHugh's paper 'On the failure of positivism' in J. Douglas (1971). The overall perspective of this chapter arises from my reading of Wittgenstein (especially *Philosophical Investigations*) and of Heidegger. For useful introductory accounts of Heidegger's position, see W. B. Macomber's *The Anatomy of Disillusion: Martin Heidegger's Notion of Truth* (1967) and R. E. Palmer's *Hermeneutics: Interpretation Theory in Schleiermacher, Dilthey, Heidegger and Gadamer* (1969) (which also includes a discussion of the work of one of Heidegger's students – Hans-Georg Gadamer).

My discussion of Zimmerman's study is taken from his Ph.D. dissertation 'People work and paper work' (1966). For a more accessible version, see his 'The practicalities of rule-use' in Douglas (*op. cit.*) and my own paper 'Accounts of organizations: organizational "structures" and the accounting process', in John McKinlay (ed.), *Processing People: Case Studies in Organization Behaviour* (1974).

5

Reading: the production of sense

Read (1) To take in the sense of, as of language . . .
(2) To interpret, hence to foresee or to foretell. (*Webster's Collegiate Dictionary*, fifth edition)

One approaches a definition of 'reading' with embarrassment. 'Reading' is, after all, what we already know how to do; it is what you are doing here and now. The kind of obviousness which this activity has for us is, if anything, confirmed when we turn to the dictionary and see 'to read' defined as 'to take in the sense of'. This, clearly, is what you are doing now; you are reading my text in order 'to take in the sense of' my words. By applying yourself to the pages I have written, you are seeking to find out what I am 'getting at'.

Definition (2) on the other hand, strikes one as somewhat strange. What has reading got to do with 'foreseeing' or 'foretelling'? And then one remembers that palms, like books, can be read. Since fortune-telling is clearly not the same kind of activity as reading a book, we now understand the reason why there are two different definitions. Each definition corresponds to a separate activity. To read (a book) is to let the author's words form impressions on one's mind, to follow where the text leads, to receive the meaning which it offers. To read (a palm) is to treat ill-defined lines on a hand as an opportunity to make a prediction

G

which will *impose* one's own sense on to the material. Instead of drifting where the text takes us, we lead and produce our meanings. The former activity seems to be essentially *passive* – reading a book is accepting the sense which its words impose upon us. The latter is essentially *active* – when we 'read' a palm, we *produce* sense through the patterns that we discover.

Our ability to separate these two kinds of reading, the one passive ('telling' the way it is), the other active ('foretelling'), expresses our security in the adoption of the passive role when we read a text. Yet this version of reading (a text) could have been otherwise – it is merely conventional:

> I knew of an uncouth region whose librarians repudiate the vain and superstitious custom of finding a meaning in books and equate it with that of finding a meaning in dreams or in the chaotic lines of one's palm ... books signify nothing in themselves. ('The Library of Babel', in Borges, 1970, p. 80)

The short story from which I have taken this passage is about a library which contains all the books which it is possible to produce from all the words in every language. For centuries, Borges tells us, men have walked its galleries, trying to discover the eternal truths that, somehow, somewhere, must be written there. Each gallery has its own librarians who offer their own version of the library's contents. On one such gallery is to be found the 'uncouth region' to which Borges refers. Here 'finding a meaning in books' is merely a 'vain and superstitious custom', equivalent to finding sense in dreams or in lines on a palm.

In equating reading a book with reading a palm, Borges implies that our version of reading is entirely conventional. If books (like palms) 'signify nothing in themselves', then we are always imposing our own sense on books. Whatever we read, we are always engaged in the active production of sense.

To approach a book intending to 'take in' its 'sense' is to forget the activity of reading. Indeed, the very passivity which this suggests is nothing more than the reader's election, his active production of sense. How have we become so forgetful? How might we re-member our forgetfulness? Here Castaneda's accounts give us an occasion to address important questions and in addressing them, to locate our-selves.

Classification and bias

In his introduction, Castaneda reports that after he had voluntarily discontinued his apprenticeship, he considered arranging his field notes 'in a systematic way':

> As the data I had collected were quite voluminous, and included much miscellaneous information, I began by trying to establish a classification system. I divided the data into areas of related concepts and procedures and arranged the areas hierarchically according to subjective importance – that is, in terms of the impact that each of them had had on me. (p. 19)

This division of the data produced a classification in terms of the uses of hallucinogenic plants; procedures and formulas used in sorcery; acquisition and manipulation of power objects; uses of medicinal plants; songs and legends. However, Castaneda tells us that he immediately felt dissatisfied by this scheme:

> Reflecting upon the phenomena I had experienced, I realized that my attempt at classification had produced nothing more than an inventory of categories; any attempt to refine my scheme would therefore yield a more complex inventory. That was not what I wanted. (*ibid.*)

Now Castaneda's problem ('that was not what I wanted') resides, I take it, in the self-enclosed nature of any inventory of categories. Categories are self-enclosed because they relate back to the interpretive framework from which they derive rather than relating forward to the 'objects' which they are used to define. For instance, what we see in a bunch of apples depends upon whether our frame of reference is scientific, artistic or nutritional. Even within such frames there are a multitude of inventories of categories that we *might* use to classify. Should we try (like Castaneda) to 'refine' our scheme, we would only produce a more complex inventory, relating back to our own frame of reference.

Don Juan alluded to our similarity as beginners through incidental comments about his incapacity to understand his teacher during his own apprenticeship. Such remarks led me to believe that to any beginner, Indian or non-Indian, the knowledge of sorcery was rendered incomprehensible by the outlandish characteristics of the phenomena he experienced. Personally, as a Western man, I found these characteristics so bizarre that it was virtually impossible to explain them in terms of my own everyday life, and I was forced to the conclusion that any attempt to classify my field data in my own terms would be futile. (pp. 19-20)

For Castaneda, the 'outlandish' or 'bizarre' characteristics of the phenomena that occurred in don Juan's world relative to the world of Castaneda's everyday life, meant that any Western scheme of classification 'would be futile'. Note that this passage does not deny the validity of classification *of* and *for* members of the same culture – it is simply that classifications do not work in the same way when taken outside a culture.

Given these difficulties, Castaneda elects to examine don Juan's knowledge 'in terms of how he himself understood it' (p. 9). However, he recognizes that more significant than any divergence of content is the differing order of conceptualization which seems to separate the two of them. Castaneda's 'first task', therefore, is to examine don Juan's method of conceptualization:

In trying to reconcile my own views with don Juan's, however, I realized that whenever he tried to explain his knowledge to me, he used concepts that would render it 'intelligible' to him. As those concepts were alien to me, trying to understand his knowledge in the way he did placed me in another untenable position. Therefore, my first task was to determine his order of conceptualization. (p. 20)

Yet in what sense, if any, is Castaneda's book an account of *don Juan's* order of conceptualization? Here we have an account, written in English, which seeks to make a replica of how a Yaqui Indian himself understands his knowledge. Yet the problematic of the book can in no way express don Juan's concerns. For Castaneda must seek to *explicate* an 'order of conceptualization' which to don Juan is not at all in need of explication. We express our competent membership of some community precisely in our ability to make out 'what's what' without conscious reference to a conceptual scheme. No doubt we could if required draw up such a scheme, but such an activity would be divorced from the

realities of our everyday lives and would bear an unknown relation
to actual instances. Indeed, our competences would only really
be properly exhibited in our ability to relate the scheme to the
unfolding contingencies of actual settings.

So the formulation of abstract rules is not a routine concern
of our everyday lives. We only feel obliged to define an 'order
of conceptualization' when faced with evidences of behaviour
which seem to be thoroughly strange. At such moments, we probe
what is bizarre for us with questions that seek to understand the
source of this strangeness. Yet our questions are addressed to a
member of a community who, because he finds such behaviour
utterly mundane, would never himself ask such 'obvious' questions.
Indeed, perhaps only when we no longer feel the need to question
what is routine for our community, but understand the world
without continual reference to the location of any event within
an 'order of conceptualization', have we understood as members
of that community understand. But here again we understand
and make classifications *of* and *for* members of the same community – only this time our understandings are of and for the
Yaqui, rather than *of* and *for* Westerners. Even within our society,
the abstract, theoretical frame of reference which classifications
like Castaneda's 'Structural Analysis' exemplify, are written for
sub-communities concerned with what they take to be 'analytic'
issues. And the degree of congruence between the 'analytic'
concerns of scientists and the practical concerns of lay members
of their society is routinely very slight. Indeed, scientists distinguish
their sub-community precisely by their own methodic distancing
from everyday problems and everyday preconceptions of the
orderly character of the world.

This kind of understanding allows us to produce a particular
sense from Castaneda's cautionary note at the beginning of his
'Structural Analysis'.

Throughout this entire work, meaning has been rendered as I
understood it. (p. 101)

The kind of disclaimer that I hear here is two-fold. First, Castaneda cannot help but make sense of don Juan's teachings in terms
of the everyday knowledge of 'the way things really are' that
exemplifies his membership of a Western society. He cannot but

help, for instance, view the sensation of human flight as a strange,
if potentially explicable, experience (i.e. as 'curious' but as none
the less intelligible, by reference to the hallucinogenic impact of
drugs, 'brainwashing', etc.). Second, Castaneda is writing not
simply as a layman with a tale to tell, but as a student of anthropology committed to the concepts and analytical schemes of his
trade. So when he writes, 'meaning has been rendered as *I* understood it', the 'I' can be heard as referring not simply to Castaneda's
bodily form or to his particular biographical experiences, but to
his existence as a Western man committed to that version of
Western thought which expresses itself as 'anthropology'.

As any Western man, Castaneda experiences don Juan's world
as 'outlandish', 'bizarre' and 'alien'. As a student of anthropology,
Castaneda feels committed to thematize this 'difference' by producing a classificatory scheme. Such a scheme will systemize don
Juan's teachings through a classification which separates and
relates in a logical form each diverse element.

So, as a Western man and an anthropologist, Castaneda renders
meaning 'as I understood it':

> At certain points extraneous classificatory items are necessary
> in order to render the phenomena understandable. And, if such
> a task was to be accomplished here, it had to be done by zig-
> zagging back and forth from the alleged meanings and classi-
> ficatory devices of the apprentice. (p. 190)

Notice how Castaneda addresses his experiences as 'phenomena'
and adopts techniques in order 'to render [them] understandable'.
This very conception of his experiences is itself a 'rendering' – a
way of treating them in which they are produced as 'data' for
scientific interpretation. So, in finding his experiences 'outlandish',
Castaneda's 'I' is probably the 'I' of any Western man. In going
on to produce 'classificatory devices' which will serve as a 'structural analysis', Castaneda's 'I' becomes the 'I' of any member
of the anthropological community. Instead of ignoring the 'outlandish' character of what seems to have happened to him, or
of expressing his re-collections in a poetic form, or even in
simply the 'reminiscences' which constitute the first part of his
book, Castaneda elects to 'render the phenomena understandable'
by means of a set of 'classificatory devices'. In doing so, he

produces his 'I', he locates him-self as any member of the Western anthropological community.

To speak seriously as a candidate-member of such a community is to show one's commitment to the production of descriptions and explanations which exemplify scientific standards. Rather than 'jump to conclusions', the scientist must carefully sift and assemble a corpus of facts (Castaneda's 'data'). Given those facts, he must engage in a recognizably rule-guided search for explanation, in which candidate-hypotheses are critically reviewed in the light of the available data. Only then can tentative conclusions be offered. Such conclusions, as all scientists recognize, stand to be refuted by further data. The community only demand that they should be based on demonstrably *plausible* inferences, not (in the fullness of time) necessarily *correct* inferences.

In all this, the potentially damning indictment of a description or explanation is that it represents not the facts but the biases of the author. Instead of properly mirroring the character of the objects of his enquiry, such an author's account tells the reader more about the former's prejudices than about the 'data'. Examine Castaneda's following statement in the light of this problem:

> In spite of all the effort I have put forth to render these concepts as faithfully as possible, their meaning has been deflected by my own attempts to classify them. (p. 189)

The aim for Castaneda, for the scientific community, is to repro-duce 'faithfully' the character of the objects of their enquiry – 'to render [them] as faithfully as possible'. Yet always in this attempt at 'faithful' rendering lurks the danger that, however 'unbiased' the observer, the very act of research may affect the materials being studied – 'their meaning [may be] deflected by[the scientist's] own attempts to classify them'.

Castaneda's use of the term 'deflected' to re-present the relation between his own text and the component concepts of don Juan's knowledge implies for me a clear expression of a commitment to a familiar version of reading. I hear in Castaneda's statement of his problem (the possibility of 'deflection'), a version of reading as that which seeks, in the words of the dictionary, 'to take in the sense of [something]'. For readings to be 'deflected' from their topic by the conceptual schemes of the author ('by my own attempts to classify') implies that the aim of interpretation (reading) is always, unshakeably, to depict *accurately* that of which it speaks. Given this aim 'to render these concepts as faithfully as possible', the problem at once arises for Castaneda of the intrinsic difficulties of his subject-matter and of the danger of his own biases preventing an objective account of the phenomena to which his text refers.

Let us consider afresh this version of reading – we might equally say version of writing. Castaneda's use of the word 'faithfully' to refer to his rendering, immediately suggests a moral dimension to the character of his enterprise. 'Faithfulness' resonates with showing 'good faith'; to write or to act 'faithfully' is to exemplify the 'moral life' in what one does. To what does one show 'faith' when one seeks to write 'as faithfully as possible'?

I hear, in Castaneda's text, his election to display his morality in and through his determination to represent 'faithfully' don Juan's teachings, while recognizing the influence of his own understandings – but seeking to minimize them. His text is to be seen as moral, then, because its author's aim is to stick to the 'facts', to recognize the potential of bias on his part and to make us aware of it. His text thus becomes moral because any reader can recognize the author's attempts to reproduce 'faithfully' the phenomena of which his text speaks and, hence, to exclude himself from the writing. Of course, such attempts, we all know, are never entirely successful – biases will keep on cropping up. Nevertheless, we feel we ought to stand back and applaud such an attempt 'to render these concepts as faithfully as possible'.

Yet, even in recognizing the author's activities as the basis for moral assessment, we have shifted the grounds of morality away from the 'data' and towards the writer. Castaneda's statement of his 'effort . . . to render these concepts as faithfully as possible' is a moral affirmation; not because he is faithful to concepts – if this were the affirmation alone, then one might well ask: Why be faithful to concepts? *Rather, Castaneda's statement exemplifies that, for him, it is faithful to be faithful to concepts.* So, in seeking to write 'as faithfully as possible', one shows commitments not to any data but to a version of good speech.

Such a version of good speech is displayed in the production of a text which reads as properly method-ical. A text which displays that, since any member of a particular (common-sense, scientific) community would be committed to the same set of methods as the author, then he too might have produced much the same text. The standard of good speech is thus the presumed interchangeability of community members. Hence Castaneda has, in this case, written the text, but we (as fellow anthropologists) are to feel that he is speaking for us – since his account exemplifies a proper attention to anthropological techniques and a recognition, and attempted minimization of, personal bias. So the version of good speech which Castaneda's text exemplifies is that version in which one speaks about 'data' as any community member might – a version of speech, to repeat, in which it is faithful to be faithful to concepts (data, facts, etc.).

But, by posing the question of good speech in this way, I am doing violence to the way in which such communities understand themselves. For them, as exemplified by Castaneda, 'faithfulness' is faithfulness to data. Moral speech is speech which seeks to correspond to the data, to minimize bias. To assert that, for them, to be faithful is to be faithful to concepts, is to locate morality in the commitment of the writer to the grounds of his speech, not in the correspondence between his speech and the world. For, in wanting to speak in a way which corresponds to the world, the speaker exemplifies his moral commitment to the grounds of his speech.

Yet, in formulating the issue this way, I am re-presenting the character of good speech. Perhaps I can formulate this by reference to the notion of responsibility. For Castaneda, in my reading, to speak responsibly is 'to stick to the facts'; conversely, to wander away from the facts, to be unconsciously deflected by biases, prejudices, oversights, etc. is to be irresponsible. Now, I am not saying that I want to oppose to this a directly contrary view. For instance, to stand this position on its head, to formulate responsibility in terms of the production of a text which is informed by bias, prejudices, and so on, is, in a sense, to accept its version of the world. For, in taking a polar-opposite view, we accept the dichotomy (facts and values) upon which the former view is grounded. In a way, then, our disagreement turns out to be a deep agreement. But it is an agreement at the level of what we take to be good, or moral, speech. For notions of 'facts' and 'bias', of 'objectivity' and 'subjectivity' all resonate with a version of good speech as speech which corresponds to some-thing (the 'data', my 'state of mind', etc.). According to such a version, then, one becomes responsible for what is concretely *said* about the topic at hand. Should a text then not be a 'truthful', 'beautiful', 'entertaining' account of that topic (the relevance of each term will depend upon the community in which the author claims membership), then the text is 'bad' and the author is 'irresponsible', 'incompetent', 'prejudiced', or whatever.

Here responsibility arises, as I have said, in the author's statements 'about' his topic – in what his text 'says'. Yet, in 'saying' whatever it says, a text conceals what makes its saying possible. For instance, in writing in a way which seeks to render concepts 'faithfully', Castaneda is forgetful of the election whereby it is faithful (to show good faith) to be faithful to concepts. Equally, in formulating Castaneda's text in this manner, I am forgetful of the grounds of my own text. So each disclosure is a concealment, a concealment of the unsaid which always makes possible what is said. My writing thus becomes a kind of pointing towards the animating grounds of my own speech. It is a reading of Castaneda's text, which, like your reading of this text, is responsible for the version of good speech which it exemplifies.

If responsibility arises in the commitment which an author's text expresses to the grounds of its speech, then Castaneda becomes responsible not for the 'deflections' of meaning in his accounts, but for his election of a mode of speech in which the aim is to be 'faithful' to facts and to be ever watchful for possible 'deflections'. We, in turn, are responsible for our reading as it exemplifies a mode of speaking. So, it is not at all a question of whether we should find Castaneda's account 'accurate' or 'deflected', for this is to find morality in faithfulness to the 'facts'. Rather, what is at issue for us, as readers, is: What is it to be faithful to the facts? Whether, in short, we wish to speak Castaneda's language.

Why should we want to ask our-selves such a question? Why not speak Castaneda's language? And, anyway, is Castaneda's language so important? Is not language a means of communication? And, if so, should we not stop worrying about the character of language and get on with *using* it in order to communicate? Yet who are 'we' outside language? From what position do we take our stand – is it not already inside language?

To see language as a means, as an object (commodity) to be used, however, does indeed make good sense to us. At all times, we want to get our language into shape in order to speak more clearly or to define more rigorously the character of our world. And what does this suggest? That it is in the character of language to be manipulated in this way? Or, rather, that in our historical epoch, this is the way in which language is heard by us? And, if the latter be so, deciding to speak Castaneda's language is, indeed, a fate-ful issue. For, as Wittgenstein tells us, in playing our language-games, we always do more than merely 'happen' to choose a useful convention. Language-games have as their bed-rock a form of life, a mode of existence. So, in expressing through our writing and reading a version of good speech, we express our way of living our lives together.

The two dictionary definitions of 'to read', offered at the beginning of this chapter, hence can be an occasion to re-member our mode of existence. To read in order 'to take in the sense' implies for me an election of the kind of passive role which unconsciously sustains what is the dominant mode of life for any community. In following along with the sense of the author, we fail to re-member that we are producing that sense ourselves, or to re-call the mode of production which that sense-making exemplifies. So we do, indeed, come to 'follow the author's sense'. Not because his text speaks for itself, but because the mode of intelligibility which both his writing and our reading re-presents is *our* mode of intelligibility, *our* community's way of living its lives together. A way in which 'accurate classification' is the aim of serious writing and 'bias' its greatest threat.

Conversely, to hear a version of reading as that which 'foresees' or 'foretells' helps to remind us that seeing (vision) is only possible through the clearing of a space (a pro-vision) in which that seeing gets done. Consequently, we come to attend to what is seen only as an exemplification of a mode of seeing. It is a mode of seeing which itself makes reference to a version of good speech and good life, where all these matters – seeing, speech and life – locate themselves in what has gone before, what is here now, and what is to become.

History

I have been trying to express that the issues involved in reading
Castaneda extend much further than the apparent 'clash of
cultures' between himself and don Juan. For me, reading, as an
organized production of sense, raises the same issues whether, in
Borges's terms, the reader is reading the lines on a palm or is
trying to make sense of 'a Yaqui way of knowledge'. Each reading,
by the version of good speech which it offers, inscribes itself as a
dialogue with a tradition which precedes it. Necessarily, the
reader produces his sense out of his location in a particular
tradition, in a particular community, in a particular historical
epoch:

> All genuinely human thinking is necessarily a thinking on the
> basis of an historical situation. Any thinking which denies this
> fact is not genuinely human thinking, or else is thinking which
> fails to understand itself. (Kockelmans, 1969, p. 28)

In this passage the writer is pointing towards the historically
situated character of any understanding. Any insight into a
phenomenon can only be an insight generated by us, as we understand things here and now. So any new 'truth' expresses the kinds
of truths potentially available to us given our historical situation –
our mode of production, both economic and intellectual. The
insight re-presents where we have come from, where we are now
and (potentially) what we might become. Thinking 'fails to understand itself', it denies its human production, when it depicts its
understandings as universal and all-encompassing.

But, of course, you might argue this version of the character
of our understandings is by no means contrary to the conventional
wisdom. Scientists, for instance, present their 'findings' as merely
the state of knowledge 'at the present'. And they understand, even
encourage, later work which may well refute their 'findings'. Yet
this recognition of the provisional character of scientific knowledge
need not in itself generate reflection on the historical character
of reading and writing as opposed to a consideration of the
history of science. Such reflection, as I have been suggesting,
circles around the act of writing itself as a socially located and
socially creative production of sense; it asks in what historical

epoch does scientific knowledge take the centre of the stage as
the paradigm of all 'serious' knowledge and questions the mode
of existence which the activity of science (we might equally say
art or literature) exemplifies.

None of this is intended as a critique of the scientific enterprise.
For, to ask questions about the historical possibility of an activity
is not to destroy it but to preserve it. Neither is it to suggest that
scientists (or artists or writers) are naïve or wrong-headed to the
extent that they fail to raise such questions. For, in being good
practitioners of their craft, such self-reflection seems to be
inimical to their projects. To the extent that they reflect upon
the status of their activities, the aim of the reflection turns upon
the defence of the practices of their community from what are
seen to be attacks which might destroy the very validity of their
project. So that while there is indeed a flourishing philosophy of
science, it tends to assume what Habermas (1972) refers to as a
prohibitive function: its role is to define and protect within those
limits the status of the scientific enterprise. Because the aim of
scientific self-reflection is, *can only be*, the defence (within bounds)
of scientific activity, science:

> is philosophical only in so far as is necessary for the immuniza-
> tion of the sciences against philosophy. (*ibid., passim*)

Yet, to repeat, in asking about the mode of existence of science,
I am not seeking to engage in a polemical exercise. My concern
is only with the version of writing and reading which science
exemplifies and with its historical possibility (as, equally, my text
exemplifies a version of writing and reading, located itself in my
historical situation).

Perhaps a happier term for the enterprise which my writing
seeks to point towards, is thinking. Thinking, as I understand it,
does not polemicize because polemics, in failing to address the possibilities of the approaches that it criticizes, immediately becomes
forgetful of its own historical possibility. As Heidegger expresses it:

> Any kind of polemics fails from the outset to assume the attitude
> of thinking. The opponent's role is not the thinking role.
> Thinking is thinking only when it pursues whatever speaks
> *for* a subject. Everything said here defensively is always intended
> exclusively to protect the subject. (1968, pp. 13-14)

For Heidegger, 'the opponent's role is not the thinking role' because an opponent's acts of destruction destroy not merely the subject of the polemic but also reflection upon the possibility of the polemic itself, and legislate how, for all time, this subject must be interpreted. So the lack of historical sense of the polemicist makes him forget the precisely historical character of his own polemic. In *exhaustively* destroying his enemy, the writer conceals the *in-exhaustible* possibilities of any text and the character of his own writing as it *exhausts* a particular historical possibility.

Where next? How to approach the historically-located character of human products (texts, paintings, buildings, revolutions) *and* of our accounts of them? At least we can rest content that we are by no means in unfamiliar territory, for these topics are much worked in our tradition. Clearly, none of the answers that have been given can be *definitive* – for that would be to forget the historical situation of the enquirer himself, it would be thinking which, in Kockelmans's words, 'fails to understand itself'. But, at least we are walking a familiar path. It is a path where there are numerous guides (does this resonate with don Juan's version of 'benefactors'?) who, while they cannot provide us with the answer, can provoke us into re-membering their questions for our-selves.

I want to begin to walk this path by considering a statement about writing and art, by Sartre; not because what Sartre says is in itself important, but because a passage of his provoked questions in me which I wanted to take further. In a collection of essays, *What is Literature?*, written just after the end of the Second World War, Sartre makes this distinction between writing and painting:

> The writer can guide you and, if he describes a hovel, make it seem the symbol of social injustice and provoke your indigna-tion. The painter is mute. He presents you with *a* hovel, that's all. You are free to see in it what you like. (1965, p. 4)

In reading this passage, I bore in mind the kind of debate which Sartre saw himself as continuing. The issue which seemed to pre-occupy French intellectuals of the period was that of the relations between their 'art' and the vast social and political movements that they saw all around them. In short, for them the issue was that of the 'commitment' of their work – its Engagement.

Sartre has no doubts that the writer engages himself in such movements in his work. However, because the painter does not produce signs (significations) like the writer – which point towards the character of our world, he is not required to 'engage' himself. Like the musician or the sculptor, what he produces are simply 'things'. Things, perhaps, in Sartre's words, 'haunted by a mysterious soul' (p. 5), but things which are not signs. So, for Sartre:

> One does not paint significations; one does not put them to music. Under these conditions, who would dare require that the painter or musician engage himself? (*ibid.*)

I don't want to answer this question of Sartre's. To 'require' an artist to do anything is to legislate what he can or cannot do. It is to refuse to take seriously *his* responsibility for the mode of intelligibility which his work proposes. Yet the issue is even more important than that of legislation of the 'proper' form of human activity.

I hear in Sartre's question an affirmation that 'engagement' is something which an artist brings to his work and seeks to impose upon it. It is as if he can *choose* whether or not his work should be engaged and then must decide how that engagement should determine his topic, style, etc. Yet what is affirmed here is precisely our mundane notion of being method-ical. Method (for which, read 'engagement') is understood as some-thing brought to a text in order to structure its character. But then what would a non-methodic text (painting, piece of music) look like? Does not any work express *some* methodic character which, rather than acting as a technique, exemplifies the producer's claim to speak (paint, compose) intelligibly? Hence method is always already within the text, within its claim to speak seriously to some audience. There is no way of writing which does not display its authority, its authoritative claims and, hence, its author.

When the artist paints, just as much as when the writer writes, he affirms his engagement because he affirms him-self – the location of his being within a mode of intelligibility which itself proposes a mode of sociality.

In a paper called 'The object-world', Roland Barthes, writing
only half-a-dozen years after Sartre, uses the Dutch painters of
the seventeenth century as an occasion to enquire into the modes
of sociality that art has proposed. To look at the artist Saenredam
is, for Barthes, to be struck by an absence. One sees neither
people nor nature in his paintings. He paints almost exclusively
the interiors of empty churches reduced to beige velvet – inoffen-
sive, as Barthes puts it, as ice-cream with nuts. You only see in
these churches panelling of wood and limestone; they are entirely
unpopulated. Saenredam is almost a contemporary painter of the
absurd. He paints with love only insignificant surfaces; Barthes
suggests that here already there is the modern aesthetic of silence.

Barthes wants to read this aesthetic as an artistic convention
which expresses a mode of existence. Saenredam's art points
towards an historical epoch in which the certainties of religion and
of divine revelation were being dissolved, a time in which man
as an individual (albeit in relation to God), responsible for his
practices, responsible for his world, was being asserted in the
Reformation. Things had newly come to derive their sense in and
through human activity; objects made immediate sense only in
relation to their instrumentality for men.

Unlike the previously dominant Catholic dogma, man could
live the religious life entirely in the world and not cloistered from
its temptations. If he sinned, he was individually responsible to
his Maker; there was no Church which could absolve him. Hence
his life must be a continual round of activity – an unceasing attack
on nature so as to dominate it and, by his good works, give proof
of his eventual salvation.

In Saenredam's paintings, then, one senses that the destiny of
the Dutch countryside is to be blackened by people; to pass
from its own infinite nature to the self-enclosed completeness of
human measurement and use. Barthes writes of the man of the
period:

> There he is, therefore, at the summit of history, knowing no
> other destiny than a progressive appropriation of material
> things. There are no more limits to this humanisation [of nature]
> and, above all, no horizon. (Barthes, 1964, p. 19, my translation)

For such men all material things are significant as things *to be used*. Where food, for instance, is presented in the art of the time, it is not because the Dutch are gourmets, but because food itself is yet another instrument for men to mould and use.

Such men recognize things only in terms of their manipulation for human purposes, only as things to be controlled. When they look up towards the sky, they see neither Nature nor Beauty, they see Their Sky:

> Everything is Man's space . . . his time is overlaid with use, there is no other authority in his life than that which he imposes on the inert, in forming it and manipulating it. (*ibid.*, p. 20)

In 'imposing' his 'authority' on the world, the Dutch artist of the period was not concerned with revealing (or liberating) the essence of objects, but only with incorporating them into human life. Hence, for the artist, in so far as his work expresses his commitment to the mode of existence of his society, all enigmas are resolved (or resoluble). The world has become entirely an expression of Man's domain. The only logical problem that confronts such an artist is how to present the material-world as a kind of surface along which men can move themselves without breaking the use-value of objects.

So Saenredam expresses for Barthes an historical period (our historical period?) in which men place no limits on their appropriation of the world, a period in which all objects have their uses and their use is expressed in their exchange-value. Amsterdam itself is presented as appropriated for human use; it is to be seen as a commodity which is an icon of a commodity-society:

> All the town of Amsterdam itself seems to have been constructed in terms of this appropriation; there are here very few materials which have not been annexed for the empire of commodities. (*ibid.*, p. 22)

For such a community, all objects are to be depicted as manipulated or as being prepared for their manipulation. Everything is to be patiently weighed as a commodity, as property. And this weighing extends not only to objects but to men themselves. The appropriation of nature appropriates human beings themselves in terms of their exchange-value. The two classes (patrician and peasant) re-presented in paintings of the period are distinguishable

H

not only by their having a different social standing but, because of their varied exchange-value, they are painted as distinct human beings. The peasants of the artist Van Ostade, Barthes tells us, invariably have their faces averted. They seem incomplete creatures, sketches of men somehow fixed in an earlier stage of human evolution:

> This under-class of man is never depicted from the front, which would suppose that they are worth at least a glance; that privilege is reserved for the patricians or for cows, the totem-animal and nourisher of the Dutch nation. . . . As the monkey is separated from man, the peasant is here distanced from the bourgeois. (*ibid.*, p. 24)

Peasants are not the only un-people for such an artist; the women of the patricians are equally deprived of their humanity, are no longer individual persons. Indeed, women are usually ignored in the paintings of the period. Where depicted, they are shown as governors of charitable institutions, accountable only for money.

In all this, are we really to believe that artists like Saenredam or Van Ostade are, in Sartre's term, 'mute'? Is not their art also a signification; does it signify nothing? Or, alternatively, as we look at the faces of Van Ostade, are we confronted by the artist's 'confession', by his expression of his commitment to the mode of life of his society and, ultimately, by his display of self as a functionary of such a society?

However we answer these questions, whether we even think them worth raising, we too, 'inescapably' express our-selves. Contrary to Sartre, I believe that *neither* the writer nor the artist guides us. We guide our-selves. So, a painting just as a text, is a social sign embedded in an artist's social production of sense – itself an expression of a possible mode of existence (Barthes writes in the same paper of a 'possible history of faces' concerned with the signification which portraits express in different times, in different places). But how we read that sign expresses not the artist but our-selves.

Barthes concludes his essay by asking whether his readers have ever thought what happens when a portrait confronts its viewer face-to-face. The expression of the bourgeois Dutchman is his proof, his affirmation of him-self. Equally, your reading of that

expression is your affirmation. When the portrait confronts you,
you are forced to participate. For the gaze you see never speaks
for itself: the expression on the canvas is 'naked' – Barthes calls
it 'this look without an adjective'. Your (their) look places you,
it makes you exist by implicating you in the mode of existence
which your look proposes.

Of course, our look never exhausts the possible 'looks'. There
are no *ultimate* looks, only historical looks. Yet Barthes sees in
these portraits the expressions of men who would suspend history
in their perfectly happy bourgeois world, a world in which men
disencumbered of God, assert their absolute mastery over all
things. Perhaps we seek to suspend history too, as we cling to
the certainties of our mode of existence as the unchallenged basis
for all our attempts to make sense?

Writing/reading

Both here and in Chapter 2 I have been implying the production
of sense involved in both writing and reading. Consequently, the
very separation of the two notions can no longer be tolerated, for
it implies a division of labour between the (active) writer and the
(passive) reader. Yet, because of its productive character, reading
is itself an act of writing, as writing is an act of reading. Neither
writer nor reader pictures a world of raw data. Rather the writer-
reader always expresses his world and, thereby, himself:

> the artist installs himself in a space carefully emptied of any
> look other than his own. Now, all art which has only two
> dimensions, that of the work and that of the spectator, can
> only create a *platitude*, since it is only the seizure of a shop-
> window display by a peeping-tom artist. Profundity is born
> only at the moment when the display itself slowly turns its
> shadow towards the man and begins to look at him. (Barthes,
> *ibid.*, p. 28)

Our work always 'installs' our-selves in space – a space on which
no sub-titles are written ('emptied of any look other than [our]
own'). Rather than seek to represent the world, as a 'peeping-tom'
artist who paints what any-man can see in a shop window, we
come to address, through Barthes, the possibilities of a writing/

reading whose only topic is the selves we display (re-member) in our methodic productions of sense. The writer's text requires a reader to clothe his 'nakedness'. The 'work' is the co-production of writer and reader; it is always incomplete without some reading. As Sartre puts it, in writing:

> the writer appeals to the reader's freedom to collaborate in the production of his work. . . . Thus, the book is not, like the tool, a means for any end whatever; the end to which it offers itself is the reader's. (1965, pp. 40-1)

The reader, for Sartre, 'collaborate[s] in the production of [the writer's] work'. Contrary to what he seemed to be implying in the earlier quotation, the writer does not 'guide you', in his example, by provoking your indignation. For that would be to make a book an instrument, a 'tool'. And here, at least, Sartre is saying that a book 'is not, like the tool, a means for any end whatever'. The only end to which a book offers itself is 'the reader's freedom'.

Because a book appeals to the reader's freedom, writing and reading are, for Sartre, profoundly *moral* issues. Notice Sartre's reference to the 'moral imperative' of artistic production, in the following passage:

> although literature is one thing and morality a quite different one, at the heart of the aesthetic imperative we discern the moral imperative. For, since the one who writes recognizes, by the very fact that he takes the trouble to write, the freedom of his readers, and since the one who reads, by the mere fact of his opening the book, recognizes the freedom of the writer, the work of art, from whichever side you approach it, is *an act of confidence in the freedom of men.* (*ibid.*, pp. 56-7, emphasis mine)

Grand-sounding phrases, indeed! Yet what is this 'freedom' in which writing is 'an act of confidence'? Do not the Dutch artists of the seventeenth century express *their* freedom in their depiction of a world 'annexed for the empire of commodities'? Their version of freedom is the freedom of the patrician (and his acolytes) to appropriate and manipulate all things for his own instrumental purposes; to judge every being in terms of its exchange-value and to ensure that the valuable belongs to the patrician. And how does the peasant, the under-class, express his 'freedom' in which, supposedly, the artist has confidence? The liberal expression of 'confidence' in, presumably the *essential* freedom of men, conceals and is the apology for an un-free social order – a social order in which, as Barthes notes, the under-class is less deserving of attention than the cow.

I hear in this passage, then, a version of freedom which makes sense for a society in which freedom, like everything else, is a commodity – a commodity reserved for a privileged class. It is, indeed, diverting for such a class to indulge themselves by encouraging artists who set their class-members 'puzzles' in the books which they write. In setting the puzzle, the writer expresses his 'freedom'; in resolving it, in his own way, his privileged reader acknowledges the 'act of confidence' which the writer has placed in him. Each write and read for each other, *for* 'each other' are the possessors of a commodity society. But where am I getting to now? Does this mean that writing does not need to set puzzles for its reader, or that the resolution of such puzzles is always the diversion of a privileged class? Emphatically no. There is no way of writing which 'tells it like it is'. Or rather writing which claims to 'tell it' that way, to represent society, engages precisely in the 'Realist' mode which is our society's language for talking about itself – it re-presents our-selves through the mode to which we are accustomed. Further, in legislating for the reader a 'proper' reading, in claiming to clarify all puzzles, it merely conceals the possibility of both the puzzle and its 'clarification' for us, in our time, in our community.

I can find no more satisfying way of pointing to the 'puzzling' character of reading and to the mysterious possibility of writing than a passage from a short story by Borges. A character has just indicated a tall lacquered desk which he refers to as Ts'ui Pen's labyrinth and comments:

Ts'ui Pen must have said once: *I am withdrawing to write a book.* And another time: *I am withdrawing to construct a labyrinth.* Every one imagined two works; to no one did it occur that the book and the maze were one and the same thing. ('The Garden of Forking Paths', in Borges, *op. cit.*, p. 50)

In re-membering that books and mazes are 'one and the same thing', we take responsibility for the socially organized production of sense which writing and reading exemplifies. But a socially organized production of sense is *not* an activity of a free man. The mere assertion of freedom is not, in Sartre's phrase 'a moral imperative'. We are all un-free in so far as 'we' are always located in a particular historical epoch, in our community's re-collection of a tradition that always precedes it. Yet in re-membering our un-freedom, we propose a possible society other than our own. For, in so far as our activity unthinkingly espouses our society's version of freedom, it sustains the mode of existence of that society. To *address* and to seek to locate historically that version of freedom is always to challenge the way we live our lives now, because that way would seek to suspend history into a frozen bourgeois world.

And it is this which, a few pages later, Sartre comes to recognize. Consider the way in which he addresses the 'freedom' of the reader in the following passage:

> Suspended between total ignorance and all-knowingness, he [the reader] has a definite stock of knowledge which varies from moment to moment and which is enough to reveal his *historicity*. In actual fact, he is not an instantaneous consciousness, a pure timeless affirmation of freedom, nor does he soar above history; he is involved in it. (*op. cit.*, p. 63)

Revealed now is a version of reading which is far from that 'pure timeless affirmation of freedom' to which Sartre seemed to be referring in the earlier passage. The 'freedom' which any reading expresses reveals man's historicity – he does not 'soar above history; he is involved in it'. His reading affirms him-self as he re-collects it in a particular historical epoch.

Borges continues his story which I have just referred to, by telling us that the lacquered desk is opened and found to contain a sheet of paper. There is just one sentence written on it:

> I leave to the various futures (not to all) my garden of forking paths. (Borges, *ibid.*)

To produce a book is to produce 'a garden of forking paths'. Borges's text, Castaneda's text, my own text, can never speak for themselves. They confront you as naked; their 'look' is without an adjective. Each reading, by the mode of intelligibility it expresses, will propose one of our 'various futures'. A text is, then, left to the various futures which will be its readings as they re-present possible modes of existence. Perhaps these futures are finite, given where we have come from and where we are now? Perhaps when Borges writes of 'not all' the various futures, he is pointing towards both the opportunity of the writer to propose possible modes of existence (an opportunity already de-limited by his historical existence) and the certainty that not all such modes will be concretely realized?

The writer clearly cannot legislate for the possible societies that will be exemplified in the readings of his text; as historically located men who are also co-producers of their world, neither writer nor reader is passive. Yet the temptation to legislate for the reader seems inescapable. On the very same page that Sartre refers to man's involvement in history, he writes of his reader:

> He has not the ignorance of the noble savage to whom everything has to be explained on the basis of principles; he is not a spirit or a *tabula rasa*. Neither has he the omniscience of an angel or of the Eternal Father. I reveal certain aspects of the universe to him; I take advantage of what he knows to attempt to teach him what he does not know. (*op. cit.*, p. 63)

Prefacing his reference to his purpose by a recognition that his reader is neither a blank sheet, nor omniscient, Sartre takes his role (the role of the writer) to be the Revealer and the Teacher. Is this not precisely the legislation which denies the necessity for the reader to collaborate in the production of sense? Yet can writing have any other impetus than the writer's conviction that he has 'something to say' – that he can see more, or at least 'differently', than the seeing of any-man? I pose these questions not as rhetorical devices in order to show my ability to pull the rabbit out of the hat but as central, yet unresolved, issues for me.

Tradition, disclosure and concealment

I can at least tread the path along which these questions lead me (perhaps I *have* to tread it that way) with a certain security.

The 'I' that I am as writer/reader is always more than my
immediate biography. To say that 'I' exist in a particular historical
epoch is to say that I re-collect my-self only in and through a
tradition which precedes me and with which my speech (my-self)
is a dialogue. So the 'something' that I have to say, the 'difference'
that my speech expresses, has its source in nothing else than the
re-trieval of the tradition which is my text (my-self). Yet to
pursue the issue further, I must address what the notion of
'tradition' re-presents for me. Once more, Borges is helpful. In
one of his essays he examines the debate in Argentinian literary
circles about the need for a specifically Argentinian literature and
about the character of the tradition that it might exemplify.
According to the solution which, he writes, 'has become almost
instinctive', Argentinian writers should use as an archetype the
poetry of 'gauchesque' poets – poetry which, by abounding in
'local colour', the gauchos, the pampas, seeks to capture the
distinctively Argentinian gaucho 'way of life'. Yet, any comparison with the popular poetry of the gauchos themselves will
at once reveal two different idioms. For instance, the gauchesque
poets cultivate a deliberately idiomatic use of language, while
gaucho poetry is always seeking to express itself in formally correct
Spanish.

It becomes clear, then, in Borges's words, that gauchesque
poetry 'is a literary genre as artificial as any other'. The tradition
which such poets seek is not to be recovered by seeking specifically
idiomatic terms, nor by filling pages with 'local colour'. Indeed,
as he suggests, perhaps what is truly native often dispenses
entirely with 'local colour'. Borges points out, for instance,
Gibbon's curious observation that the Koran makes no reference
to camels; he goes on:

> I believe if there were any doubt as to the authenticity of the
> Koran, this absence of camels would be sufficient to prove it
> as an Arabian work . . . the first thing a falsifier, a tourist, an
> Arab nationalist would do is to have a surfeit of camels, caravans
> of camels, on every page; but Mohammed, as an Arab, was
> unconcerned: he knew he could be an Arab without camels.
> ('The Argentine Writer and the Tradition', in Borges, *op. cit.*,
> p. 215)

But, if 'local colour' (the pampas instead of camels) does not recover the tradition for the Argentinian writer, neither, Borges argues, does an attempt to ape Spanish literature, or, conversely, to eschew all things European. Specifically Spanish works resonate for him with another history, both politically and artistically distinct from Argentine history. On the other hand, how can the Argentinian writer be cut off from the history of the West in general? While Argentinian artists need not 'play at' being Europeans, their mode of discourse inescapably expresses the historical unfolding of Western life and thought. In seeking to 'cut off' himself from Europe, the writer is, then, deeply forgetful of the location of him-self in the outcomes of social and ideological disputes extending back to the pre-Socratics.

Having cleared the ground this way, Borges can pose a simple question and a simple answer:

> What is our Argentine tradition? I believe we can answer this question easily and that there is no problem here. I believe our tradition is all of Western culture, and I also believe we have a right to this tradition. . . . (*ibid.*, p. 218)

Yet, as Borges himself recognizes, this is by no means the end of the matter. Any attempt to locate, concretely, a tradition, expresses an historically-located anxiety. It re-presents a time in which writers need to seek a 'formula' which they can follow in their writings; when they need to know what does (or should) determine the character of their work. But work is never the mere *product* of technique; it exemplifies its own mode of production. Rather than develop techniques or programmes, we should listen to the programme which our very writing points towards (which our acts of production re-collect). Once again, Borges triumphantly points towards the character of such a writing:

> I believe . . . that all these *a priori* discussions concerning the intent of literary execution are based on the error of supposing that intentions and plans matter a great deal . . . I believe that if we surrender ourselves to that voluntary dream which is artistic creation, we shall be Argentine and we shall be good or tolerable writers. (*ibid.*, pp. 219-20)

The 'artistic creation' to which Borges refers in this passage has
nothing to do with that version of 'art' which would separate it
from life and measure it by 'eternal' standards: artistic modes
of production always inscribe themselves in social modes of
production. The writer produces through his retrieval of the
tradition in his time, as the reader produces in his time. Indeed,
there is a story of Borges which shows us through irony the
historical character of our production (of texts, of selves).

Borges writes of one Pierre Menard who, fascinated by *Don
Quixote*, set out to re-write it. But, as Borges tells us:

> He did not want to compose another *Quixote* – which is easy –
> but *the Quixote itself*. Needless to say, he never contemplated
> a mechanical transcription of the original; he did not propose
> to copy it. His admirable intention was to produce a few pages
> which would coincide – word for word and line for line – with
> those of Miguel de Cervantes. ('Pierre Menard, Author of the
> *Quixote*', in Borges, *op. cit.*, pp. 65-6)

How can Menard's text be the same yet different from Cervantes?
Only if we re-member that a text (what is said) points unavoidably
to what makes it possible (the unsaid). In writing *Don Quixote*
in his time, Menard re-presents the retrieval of the tradition, he
re-collects him-self here and now. Equally, as we read Menard's
text, we locate our-selves in our time – in terms of where we
have come from and what we might become. Indeed, is there
not a deep seriousness in Borges's comments about the two
texts?

> Cervantes' text and Menard's are verbally identical, but the
> second is almost infinitely richer. (More ambiguous, his
> detractors will say, but ambiguity is richness) . . . The contrast
> in style is also vivid. The archaic style of Menard – quite
> foreign, after all – suffers from a certain affectation. Not so
> that of his forerunner who handles with ease the current
> Spanish of his time. (p. 69)

Now in none of this do I feel that we have come any closer to
the issue with which I began this section. I am no closer to a
conception of 'tradition', except if Borges's gloss 'all of Western
culture' will suffice. Yet what would it look like to formulate my

(our?) tradition? Surely, it would be within the tradition itself which would grant that we could raise and answer such questions?

Yet all production discloses something. Neither I nor you would have come this far if there was nothing to be said. Concretely, my text has disclosed some of the possibilities of re-membering Castaneda. More significantly, it has pointed towards my re-collection of my-self in the possibility of recognizing such possibilities in our time. So my writing, in disclosing my mode of production, has disclosed my-self. But like any disclosure, it is also a concealment. My text, in disclosing some possibilities of reading Castaneda's book has, obviously, concealed others. More fundamentally, in its seeing (vision), it has necessarily concealed the opening of the space in which that seeing became possible (my pro-vision). That is why, like any text, my own is incomplete – it needs your reading to complete it.

But even that (or any) reading will never 'finally' complete the text. Nor will our writing/reading 'finally' disclose the 'essence' of Castaneda's text. It will not demystify Castaneda because, as Barthes has remarked, there is also 'a mythology of the mythologist'. Perhaps a further sentence of his will help us to re-member the historical character of our activities: 'What I claim', he writes, 'is to live to the full the contradiction of my time, which may well make sarcasm (irony?) the condition of truth' (*Mythologies*, Paladin: London, 1973, p. 12). In living to the full that contradiction, we remember our mode of existence – we must write or be written upon.

Bibliography

The works listed here are those cited in the text. Special recommendations for further reading are listed at the ends of chapters 2, 3 and 4.

AUSTIN, J. L. (1962), *Sense and Sensibilia*, Oxford University Press, London.

BARTHES, R. (1964), *Essais Critiques*, Editions du Seuil, Paris.

BARTHES, R. (1967), *Writing Degree Zero*, Cape, London.

BLUM, A. (1974), *Theorizing*, Heinemann Educational Books, London.

BORGES, J.-L. (1970), *Labyrinths*, Penguin, Harmondsworth.

DOUGLAS, J. (1970), *The Social Meanings of Suicide*, Princeton University Press.

DOUGLAS, J. (1971), *Understanding Everyday Life*, Routledge & Kegan Paul, London.

DURKHEIM, É. (1952), *Suicide*, Routledge & Kegan Paul, London.

DURKHEIM, É. (1964), *The Rules of Sociological Method*, trans. by S. Solovay and J. Mueller, Free Press, New York.

FILMER, P. *et al.* (1972), *New Directions in Sociological Theory*, Collier-Macmillan, London.

FILMER, P. *et al.* (forthcoming), *Stratifying Practices: Essays in Reflexive Sociology*, Routledge & Kegan Paul, London.

GARFINKEL, H. (1967), *Studies in Ethnomethodology*, Prentice-Hall, New Jersey.

HABERMAS, J. (1972), *Knowledge and Human Interests*, Heinemann, London.

HEATH, S. (1972), *The Nouveau Roman*, Elek Books, London.

HEIDEGGER, M. (1968), *What is Called Thinking*, trans. by F. D. Wieck and J. Glean Gray, Harper & Row, New York.

HEIDEGGER, M. (1971), *On the Way to Language*, Harper & Row, New York.

KOCKELMANS, J. (1969), *The World in Science and Philosophy*, Bruce, Milwaukee.

MCHUGH, P. *et al.* (1974), *On the Beginning of Social Enquiry*, Routledge & Kegan Paul, London.

MCKINLAY, J. (ed.) (1974), *Processing People: Case Studies in Organization Behaviour*, Harper & Row, New York.

MACOMBER, W. B. (1967), *The Anatomy of Disillusion*, Northwestern University Press, Evanston.

MARX, K. (1962 edn), *The Economic and Philosophic Manuscripts of 1844*, Milligan translation, International Publishers, New York.

PALMER, R. E. (1969), *Hermeneutics: Interpretation Theory in Schleiermacher, Dilthey, Heidegger and Gadamer*, Princeton University Press.

PEARS, D. (1970), *Wittgenstein*, Fontana, London.

PITKIN, H. (1972), *Wittgenstein and Justice*, Berkeley, California.

SARTRE, J.-P. (1965), *What is Literature?*, Harper & Row, New York.

SILVERMAN, D. (1974), 'Accounts of organizations', in McKinlay (ed.) (1974).

SILVERMAN, D. and JONES, J. (1975), *Organizational Work: the Language of Grading, the Grading of Language*, Collier-Macmillan, London.

WITTGENSTEIN, L. (1969 edn), *Philosophical Investigations*, trans. by G. E. M. Anscombe, Blackwell, Oxford.

WITTGENSTEIN, L. (1970 edn), *On Certainty*, Harper & Row, New York.

ZIMMERMAN, D. H. (1966), 'People work and paper work: a study of a Public Assistance Agency', unpublished doctoral dissertation, Department of Sociology, University of California.